OVER_____ A IN ADULTS: THE RESILIENT PATH

5 STEPS TO INNER TRANSFORMATION FROM INVISIBLE WOUNDS, CULTIVATE HEALTHY RELATIONSHIPS, AND EMPOWERED LIFE BEYOND ANXIETY, DEPRESSION & SHAME

SALINA CRESPIN

© **Copyright 2023 - All rights reserved.**

The content contained within this book may not be reproduced, duplicated or transmitted without direct written permission from the author or the publisher.

Under no circumstances will any blame or legal responsibility be held against the publisher, or author, for any damages, reparation, or monetary loss due to the information contained within this book, either directly or indirectly.

Legal Notice:

This book is copyright protected. It is only for personal use. You cannot amend, distribute, sell, use, quote or paraphrase any part, or the content within this book, without the consent of the author or publisher.

Disclaimer Notice:

Please note the information contained within this document is for educational and entertainment purposes only. All effort has been executed to present accurate, up to date, reliable, complete information. No warranties of any kind are declared or implied. Readers acknowledge that the author is not engaged in the rendering of legal, financial, medical or professional advice. The content within this book has been derived from various sources. Please consult a licensed professional before attempting any techniques outlined in this book.

By reading this document, the reader agrees that under no circumstances is the author responsible for any losses, direct or indirect, that are incurred as a result of the use of the information contained within this document, including, but not limited to, errors, omissions, or inaccuracies.

CONTENTS

Introduction   9

1. UNVEILING TRAUMA—THE UNSEEN WOUNDS   15
   Demystifying Trauma: A Closer Look   16
   Unraveling the Types of Trauma: More Than One Face   24
   Trauma: A Universal Experience   27

2. THE BODY'S ECHO—UNRAVELING THE PHYSICAL AND MENTAL RESPONSES TO TRAUMA   31
   The Fight, Flight, or Freeze Response   32
   The Role of the Nervous System: The Conductor of the Body's Response to Trauma   34
   The Physical Manifestation of Trauma: When the Body Speaks   36
   The Psychological Effects of Trauma   38
   Understanding Triggers   40
   Coping With Trauma Responses   42

3. JOURNEY TO RECOVERY—ONE STEP AT A TIME   47
   Acknowledging Your Trauma: The First Step Toward Healing   48
   Step 2: Patience: Understanding the Pace of Healing   50
   Step 3: Self-Love and Self-Compassion: Nurturing Your Emotional Well-Being   52
   Step 4: Leveraging Personal Strengths: You Are Stronger Than You Believe   56
   Step 5: Creating a Safe and Supportive Environment: A Sanctuary for Healing   58

4. GUIDED PATHWAYS—SEEKING
   PROFESSIONAL HEALTH FOR TRAUMA
   RECOVERY   61
   The Role of Therapy in Trauma Recovery   62
   Medication as a Supportive Tool in Recovery   65
   The Search for the Right Therapist   69

5. BOUNCING BACK—THE POWER OF
   ADAPTABILITY   75
   The Nature of Resilience: Turning Adversity
   Into Strength   76
   Building Resilience: Practical Steps to Foster
   Growth   77
   Resilience in Action: Real-Life Examples   81

   MID-BOOK REVIEW PAGE   87

6. EMPOWERMENT FROM WITHIN—
   HARNESSING YOUR INNER STRENGTH   91
   Unearthing Your Inner Strength: The
   Hidden Power Within   92
   Inner Strength in Action: Empowering Your
   Recovery   96
   Maintaining Your Inner Strength: An
   Ongoing Commitment   99

7. REBUILDING BRIDGES   105
   The Impact of Trauma on Personal
   Relationships   106
   The Path to Rebuilding Trust   109
   Communication: A Key Tool in Healing
   Relationships   111
   Seeking Professional Help for Relationship
   Challenges   113
   Cultivating New Relationships Post-Trauma   116

8. NURTURING THE SELF—THE ART OF
   SELF-CARE IN TRAUMA RECOVERY   119
   Understanding Self-Care: More Than Just a
   Buzzword   120
   Physical Self-Care: Nurturing Your Body   123

Emotional Self-Care: Tending to Your
Emotional Garden 126
Balancing Self-Care With Life's Demands 132

9. **THE SILVER LINING—EMBRACING POST-
TRAUMATIC GROWTH** 135
Unraveling Post-Traumatic Growth 136
The Five Domains of Post-Traumatic
Growth 139
Fostering Traumatic Growth: Strategies for
Transformation 142
Embracing Yourself: The Transformational
Power of Trauma 145

10. **A BRIGHTER TOMORROW—STAYING ON
THE PATH OF HEALING** 151
Staying the Course: Maintaining Progress in
Healing 152
Turning Setbacks Into Comebacks 156
The Road Ahead: Embracing an Empowered
Future 159
Your Lifelong Companion: Cultivating
Resilience 161

Conclusion 165
References 173

*To Richie Weisberg,
who struggled and is no longer struggling.*

"*I didn't have a hard time making it.
I had a hard time letting it go.*"
-Elliot Smith

INTRODUCTION

Sometimes, it only takes hearing the success of others who have walked similar paths to inspire you. Anthony exhibited behaviors that were associated with trauma since he was a young kid. Anthony expressed the trauma from his father leaving his family and finding his role model, his grandfather, dead body from suicide. He would experiment with alcohol and drugs, disappear from home, avoid attending classes, and even had to deal with the law at times. Anthony was affected to the extent that he even showed that he had suicidal thoughts, mainly based on what he would say.

Anthony attempted multiple inpatient and outpatient treatment centers that had failed. His low self-esteem habits were apparent, and his sleeping patterns were getting affected, too. He would become withdrawn, depressed, and paranoid. With help from the staff at the treatment centers, Anthony was diagnosed with bipolar disorder. This marked the beginning of Anthony's journey to recovery as he began to understand what he was going through. With having an understanding of the symptoms and having the support, it is possible to recover from trauma if you stay the course. You got this!

Salina Crespin, the author of *Overcoming Trauma in Adult: The Resilient Path*, is a resilient and tenacious individual who has personally experienced and triumphed over adversity and trauma. Through their journey, they have developed a deep understanding of trauma recovery and the power of inner healing. With a background in substance abuse counseling, Salina brings her expertise and empathy to their writing. Their passion for empowering others to overcome trauma while they find strength and healing shines through in their candid and inspiring account. Salina's personal experiences and professional knowledge make them a beacon of hope for readers seeking to overcome trauma and embrace a life of empowerment.

Before compiling this book, a general assessment of the experiences and feelings of people who have been through traumatic events was done. Based on the investigation, it was noted that many of the people, regardless of gender, struggled with recurrent memories of what happened. Such intrusive thoughts may interfere with their ability to regulate their emotions. For some, the distress associated with recurrent memories of traumatic events negatively affects their ability to interact and develop meaningful relationships with others. Such individuals highlighted that they found it difficult to rebuild the trust shattered by what they had been through. Some end up blaming themselves for what happened. *I wish I could turn back the hands of time*, some would say, with a tone that showed regret, as if the past events were under their control. To some, the trauma had gone beyond emotions and thoughts, as their physical well-being was gradually becoming compromised.

Chronic pain, insomnia, and fatigue are among the symptoms reported by trauma victims. Do you relate to any of these circumstances? If yes, then this book is a must-have in your library. It is equipped with science-backed techniques, practical steps to desired outcomes, real-life success stories, and tools that help you maintain the changes that you would have established.

This book will help you overcome the negative results of the traumatic events that you encountered in five significant ways:

- *It provides tailored coping strategies*: This will improve your ability to regulate your emotions.
- *It encourages cognitive exercises*: Cognitive workouts assist you by enhancing your concentration. This way, you can make better decisions in a timely manner. Cognitive exercises make it easier for you to deal with intrusive

thoughts that often interfere with your task completion.

- *It highlights physical wellness techniques*: Some signs and symptoms of physical distress, including pain and fatigue, can be addressed by engaging in specific exercises, some of which will be described in this book.
- *It re-nurtures trust-building strategies*: Practical nuggets that can enhance your ability to connect with others on various levels are unleashed in this guide.
- *It enhances self-forgiveness and acceptance*: Showing yourself some love and kindness is one of the effective coping strategies for trauma management. This strategy will reduce feelings of shame, self-blame, and guilt while fostering increased self-esteem and image.

In the United States alone, 70% of the adult population has been a victim of trauma at some point in their life (The National Council for Behavioral Health, n.d.). This amounts to approximately 223.4 million people.

Similarly, the Substance Abuse and Mental Health Services Administration highlighted that 51% and 61% of women and men report at least one instance of trauma in their lives (FHE Health, n.d.). These statistics show that more than half of the population is bound to deal with cases of trauma in one way or another. This also suggests that you are not alone in the journey of recovering from trauma. As you read, you will realize that so many people who have encountered traumatic events are bouncing back. Therefore, you stand equal chances of making it, and you will!

1

UNVEILING TRAUMA—THE UNSEEN WOUNDS

When she found a job at this new school, Ms. Denver quickly noticed this little girl who handled herself relatively differently. From this new teacher's observation, the other teachers, classmates, and schoolmates had become used to the girl's secluded behavior. Ms. Denver described the girl as unsociable and easily irritated by the few people who inquired about her behavior. The new teacher took it upon herself to discover what was happening to the girl, whom she later found to be Rose.

What an irony—a rose can be so beautiful yet thorny simultaneously. Approaching Rose wasn't an easy endeavor, yet it was worthwhile to Ms. Denver, who once worked as a counselor with children who had gone through various traumas. What she then found out confirmed her assumptions—Rose had lost her whole family to a fire outbreak, and she was the only survivor. She was lucky because she had a sleepover right next door where her childhood friend stayed. "I can still see the flames," Rose told Ms. Denver as tears engulfed both eyes. Ms. Denver realized that Rose had deep wounds that people could not see just at a glance.

Sadly, she is not the only one who has such *unseen wounds*. You might have had your share of hurtful life experiences and can't seem to recognize yourself anymore. Could it be that a friend, relative, or sibling is failing to cope, and you don't know how to help them? Whatever the case, this chapter will unleash what you need to know to understand what trauma is.

DEMYSTIFYING TRAUMA: A CLOSER LOOK

Did you know that trauma is the Greek word for *wound*? Generally, trauma can be described as an emotional or psychological response to scary or stressful events that may have happened in the past. Good examples of such events include accidents, violence, or assaults of any form, all of which can cause inner wounds. This shows that trauma can result from seemingly small events to relatively big ones in the eyes of the observer. However, the theoretical extent of the traumatizing event does not determine how people are affected by it. For example, *smaller* events could cause more trauma than the *bigger* ones.

People respond differently to similar traumatic events, which determines how much they are affected. Some can quickly go over what happened, while others sustain long-lasting effects. It is important to note that many factors determine an individual's ability to cope after a traumatic scenario. For instance, those who get timely and appropriate support might recuperate more easily. If traumatized individuals do not get help on time, their emotional, psychological, and physical well-being are affected. Statistics show that approximately 20% end up being victims of post-traumatic stress disorder (PTSD) (Al Jowf et al., 2022).

The Visible Signs and Effects of Trauma

A person can assume they are fine, even when they are going through trauma. Such people still are in the denial stage, where they find it difficult to accept what happened. As a result, they continuously tell themselves that they are okay. However, you can tell that one is undergoing trauma by observing certain signs that we will discuss in this section.

Effects on Mental Health

Trauma can lead to stress, which can have more devastating effects if experienced over long periods (SAMHSA, 2022). The prolonged stress from trauma can cause anxiety, depression, or even PTSD. Usually, the anxiety is associated with flashbacks of the traumatic events. Such scenarios may significantly interfere with how you focus on completing tasks and responsibilities, negatively affecting your overall performance.

Effects on Physical Health

Some victims of trauma report heart, digestive system, skin, and kidney issues, which are more likely to have resulted from stress. Sleeping patterns are also affected. Typically, sleep involves different stages that one should go through, one of which is rapid eye movement (REM). The REM sleep stage involves storing and processing memories (Khiron Clinics, 2022). Therefore, the fact that trauma interferes with this stage of sleep negatively affects how you deal with memories associated with traumatic events.

Memories of traumatic events may make it difficult for you to relax, negatively affecting the quality and quantity of your sleep. Such was the case with Kimi, who is a Native American lady aged 35 years old. When she was 16, Kimi was group-raped on her way home from school. The memories of what happened have stayed with her for this long, to the extent that she never feels safe, whether alone or with others. Kimi feels that the event might repeat itself, significantly compromising her ability to relax.

Here is what Kimi has to say (Substance Abuse and Mental Health Services Administration, 2014):

I have a hard time relaxing. I can easily get startled if a leaf blows across my path or if my children scream while playing in the yard. The best way I can describe how I experience life is by comparing it to watching a scary, suspenseful movie—anxiously waiting for something to happen, palms sweating, heart pounding, on the edge of your chair.

It's difficult for anyone to engage in a deep sleep when they are feeling this way.

Effects on Emotional Health

Trauma-related stress may also affect your emotional health in two significant ways (Center for Substance Abuse Treatment [US], 2014). First, it causes emotional dysregulation, characterized by losing control of your major emotions, like sadness, anger, anxiety, and shame. Usually, emotional dysregulation is short-lived in adults than it is in children. Some try to rectify the situation by engaging in self-regulatory behaviors, which may include disordered eating and substance abuse. Second, emotional dysregulation may result in numbing, which describes a situation where your emotions are relatively detached from your memories, thoughts, and behaviors. In this case, you can't attach any emotions to anything you experience, not even past traumatic events.

The Center for Substance Abuse Treatment highlighted one case of a female, whom we will call Shanon. Her mother's boyfriend had abused Shanon at a young age.

Shanon's trauma led her to incidences of substance abuse and aggressive behavior. When interviewed, Shanon showed that she had gone through a level of numbing. She said, "I learned long ago not to wear emotions on my sleeve."

If you feel like you don't have feelings, you are not the only one. What you are experiencing highlights the extent to which you have been affected by the traumatic event that you experienced.

Effects on Social Health

Trauma tends to affect the extent to which you can trust other people. Being untrusting of people is especially true if your experiences involve intentional harm from people, as was the case with Kimi. It might take time to believe that not everyone intends to harm you. The inability to trust the people around you may reflect your unwillingness to develop sustainable relationships. For example, it becomes more difficult for you to create and maintain friendships.

Misconceptions Around Trauma

The variations in the causes, effects, and responses to trauma make this condition quite challenging to understand. The many different causes and effects partly explain the existence of many misconceptions that are associated with it, some of which we will discuss in this section:

Only Weak People Struggle With Trauma

Even the strongest people can succumb to trauma, considering its complexity. Besides, facing trauma shows that you have accepted your fears, expressed your emotions, and are willing to get assistance. These are some of the most vital attributes that people can ever possess. They don't exhibit weakness. Therefore, the fact that you are going through trauma reflects your strength, not weakness. It shows that you are a normal human being who has emotions.

Only Life-Threatening Events Cause Trauma

Indeed, life-threatening events such as accidents, natural disasters, and wars are among the most common causes of trauma. However, this does not rule out other factors such as divorce, which are not a direct threat to your life, yet they negatively affect your self-worth, sense of belonging, and, sometimes, your financial security. The complexity of events emphasizes that trauma is quite subjective, considering that divorce can traumatize one person, yet another person might see it as a form of relief. Therefore, if you are traumatized by an event that doesn't seem to affect the next person, that does not make you abnormal or weak. You are unique in your own way, and events affect you differently.

Nothing Good Comes Out of "Trauma"

Trauma has many adverse effects that overwhelm the possibility of any positivity. However, have you ever heard of post-traumatic growth (PTG)? PTG refers to strength and resilience that develop as a result of the harsh situations that you may have gone through. Over time, people who bounce back from traumatizing events tend to attain amazing resilience. They become strong enough to survive anything that they face in life.

Think of Darrell Hammond, who experienced abuse during his childhood (Inspire Malibu, 2021). Hammond had to deal with alcohol and drug abuse for many years due to what he had gone through. However, he overcame this and advocated for therapy and treatment for other people going through similar experiences. Hammond has since lived a sober lifestyle and is a role model to many people.

There are many other celebrities whom you probably admire today who came out victorious after serious traumatic events. These include Oprah Winfrey, Will Smith, Demi Moore, Tyler Perry, and Hilary Swank (Robinson, 2021). These celebrities are good evidence that you can still make it in life, regardless of what you have been through.

You Should Quickly Get Over It

You might have heard this statement often: "You should quickly get over it." There is no one-size-fits-all way of dealing with trauma. Depending on how traumatized you are, it can take a short or long time. If it takes long before you heal, it is still okay.

You Will Get Over It if You Talk About It More Often

Talking about what you went through could be helpful, but this is not always the case. Talking about trauma is especially true if you recite the traumatic incidents without the relevant guidance and support from a trauma specialist. If this happens, talking about what happened may have similar effects to experiencing it again, which may cause more negative effects.

It is important to note that memories that are associated with trauma are not stored as *long-term* memories by your brain (Stanton, 2021). When events are kept as long-term memories, your mind gradually gets over it as it recognizes that the incident is now in the past. The fact that traumatic events are not stored as long-term memories means that each time you talk about them, it may feel like a rewind of what happened. You can even cry and feel angry, bored, frustrated, or irritated as if the incident was happening right now.

UNRAVELING THE TYPES OF TRAUMA: MORE THAN ONE FACE

Trauma assumes different faces, and each type has unique characteristics and effects, further determining the treatment and recovery strategies that should be undertaken. Recognizing the various types of trauma is vital to understanding and empathizing with survivors. Please note that it is possible to transition from one type of trauma to another as time progresses. Trauma is classified into three types that we will explain in this section.

Acute Trauma

Trauma that is associated with one highly stressful event is referred to as acute. For example, if you experience trauma after seeing a fatal accident happen, you might experience acute trauma. Life-threatening events can trigger acute trauma. If not appropriately addressed, acute trauma can cause serious mental health problems over time. This type of trauma is often associated with a mental health condition called acute stress disorder (ASD), whose signs and symptoms may become evident as early as three days after the event in question. ASD can stick around for about a month.

If you are experiencing acute trauma, you may benefit from cognitive behavioral therapy (CBT), which helps you to process and evaluate your thoughts and feelings about the traumatic event (National Institute of Mental Health,

2022). CBT describes a scenario where you talk about your experiences under the guidance of a trauma expert to change your perceptions and, ultimately, the way you behave.

Chronic Trauma

With chronic trauma, scary and stressful experiences occur repeatedly. Chronic trauma often occurs with physical and sexual abuse, where the perpetrators regularly attack their victims. Other experiences that can be classified as traumatic include domestic violence and poverty. In addition to being a threat to physical, mental, and emotional well-being, chronic trauma may also gradually reduce the self-esteem of the affected individual. Chronic trauma may also cause hopelessness that leads to detrimental changes in behavior. This is why some substance abuse cases emanate from exposure to chronic trauma. Some affected individuals may become extremely irritable.

Chronic trauma victims usually require longer-term treatment strategies like trauma-focused cognitive behavioral therapy (TF-CBT). Eye movement desensitization and reprocessing (EMDR) is also another effective strategy. EMDR is a therapy that helps one to deal with the aftermath of a traumatic incident, and it mainly focuses on transforming the memory rather than the feelings, thought patterns, or how you respond to situations. TF-CBT is a short-term therapy that usually involves the family to give you better support that assists you in healing.

Complicated Trauma

As the name suggests, this type of trauma is quite complex. First, complicated trauma happens when one experiences multiple stressful events unlimitedly. Let's suppose that one loses a sibling who was taking care of them in a natural disaster before they start staying with a couple who abuses them. If poverty is also a factor in the scenario, this becomes a complicated trauma case. In cases where chronic trauma stretches for too long, it upgrades to the *complicated* version. This often happens with abandonment trauma, where one would have experienced neglect in their childhood.

Abuse can also transit into complicated trauma if it continues over a long time. Applying a combination of therapeutic approaches effectively addresses complicated trauma cases. Some approaches you can combine include somatic experiencing and dialectical behavior therapy (DBT). Somatic experiencing is based on noticing the bodily sensations associated with the situations or events that traumatize you. The more you become acquainted with such sensations, the better oriented you become toward healing. You can think of DBT as another form of talking therapy that is tailor-made for individuals who experience intense emotions.

TRAUMA: A UNIVERSAL EXPERIENCE

Trauma affects people of all ages, backgrounds, and walks of life. Before the COVID-19 pandemic, the World Health Organization reported that 70% of people have had traumatic experiences in their lives, based on the findings from 24 countries (Staglin, 2022). Such trauma occurs at home, workplaces, schools, or even online. There are reports that some individuals experience trauma as a result of malicious comments during online dating (Sudderth, 2023). On the other hand, statistics from the US showed that approximately two million people are affected by trauma that emanates from workplace violence every year (Staglin, 2022). Although anyone can experience trauma, the extent of the effects varies between individuals due to various factors, which include the following:

- *Prior health mental conditions*: Trauma is more likely to have more significant effects if you already have other mental issues, such as depression.
- *Lack of social support*: When you go through a traumatic experience alone, dealing with the effects might be more difficult.
- *Cultural beliefs and issues*: Some cultures may stigmatize mental health issues, making it more difficult for individuals affected by trauma to seek help.

- *The size of the trauma*: The size of the trauma is determined by three factors which are *intensity, frequency,* and *duration*. The intensity of the traumatic event depends on the pain involved, the possibility of death, and the level of violence involved, among other factors. A traumatic event that repeats itself many times is more likely to have devastating effects than a one-off one, though this is not always the case. The trauma that sticks around for prolonged periods may have more resounding effects on victims when compared to short-term ones.
- *The resulting post-trauma hardships*: After a traumatic event, hardships such as job loss, disability, stigma, and death of loved ones may result. Such aftereffects may impact your ability to recuperate and the rate at which you can do so.
- *Events or monuments associated with the trauma*: Let's compare an accident that takes place on Christmas day versus the one that happens any other day. The former is more challenging to get over than the latter. So, when things make you remember what happened, dealing with the trauma can be more difficult.

Recognizing and understanding that trauma is universal helps us foster empathy to support each other. There is no need to stigmatize trauma survivors as this only aggravates their situations. If someone else is going through trauma, be there for them because trauma is not a sign of weakness or a character flaw; it's a human experience that calls for compassion and support. Having understood this, there is a need to understand the physical and mental responses to trauma. Get more details in Chapter 2.

2

THE BODY'S ECHO—UNRAVELING THE PHYSICAL AND MENTAL RESPONSES TO TRAUMA

How you respond to trauma is primarily a result of how your mind has become accustomed to dealing with stressful situations. When you are constantly subjected to trauma, you may develop a particular way of responding to similar scenarios to cope. Your brain stores events that previously happened and uses them to determine how to react to similar ones should they occur in the future.

As time passes, your body becomes accustomed to certain behaviors in the face of particular triggers. If you were bullied as a child, you are more likely to develop a timid nature that quickly gives in to outward threats. Being timid is because the *fear* will be engraved in your mind, determining how you behave or react to situations. In this chapter, we will explore how the body and mind respond to trauma to facilitate recognizing appropriate responses while also ushering you through your healing process.

THE FIGHT, FLIGHT, OR FREEZE RESPONSE

Your instinct to confront danger, flee from it, or stay rooted to the spot is your body's response to dealing with threats. This response, often described as *fight* or *flight*, is triggered by the signals your brain sends to your body. Traumatic experiences in people tend to cause extreme responses to the things they face. When you have been exposed to chronic trauma, especially in your childhood, your response to something you consider a potential threat will likely be exaggerated.

- *The fight response*: If you were a victim of verbal abuse or constant scolding as a child, you are more likely to grow up thinking that anyone who corrects you is attacking you. As a result, you may become too defensive or overly nice so that you can appease the other person. The tendency to act in these extremes may adversely affect your health in the near future, as your brain becomes constantly hyperactive in anticipation of a perceived threat to your peace. Overreaction in self-defense is synonymous with the *fight* response.
- *The flight response*: It is also possible to be overly passive toward matters that you do not appreciate.

You can think of the *flight* response as avoidance, which tends to affect your level of assertiveness. Now, agreeing to something because you are afraid of offending someone when you know you are against it can reflect a lack of interest in developing honest relationships. This affects the social aspects of your life.

The experiences that you go through in childhood will stick in your mind for long. This is because when you are young, your brain is still developing and is more likely to hold on to what it is exposed to. According to Dr. Nadine Burke Harris, childhood trauma significantly affects brain development. She also highlights that it affects the hormonal and overall immune systems. Childhood trauma is also believed to increase the risk of lung cancer and heart disease while significantly reducing life expectancy by up to 20 years (The Burke Foundation, 2019).

Such negative effects are profound and cannot be ignored. Adverse childhood experiences (ACEs) were closely linked to chronic diseases and premature death in a study conducted by CDC-Kaiser (The Burke Foundation, 2019).

However, despite the potential health challenges ACEs pose, there is much hope for you to excel and succeed in life. A strong support base of family, friends, and other caregivers can act as a cushion against the impact of childhood trauma on your personal development. Capacity building for caregivers and guardians also helps you to develop into an adult with the chance to live a normal life just like anybody else who has not gone through ACEs.

THE ROLE OF THE NERVOUS SYSTEM: THE CONDUCTOR OF THE BODY'S RESPONSE TO TRAUMA

When you go through traumatic experiences, your central nervous system largely determines how much you will react. Your nervous system is made up of your brain, spinal cord, and a network of nerves. The brain is the central controlling organ. The components of the nervous system form a network that relays messages from the brain to the rest of your body. The central nervous system controls all your body activities, including breathing and heart rate. Traumatic events tend to increase both the breathing and heart rates due to the nervous system being triggered. This is why you may breathe faster and more shallowly when someone makes you angry.

Your body is regulated by the nervous system to function involuntarily. This system is divided into the parasympathetic and the sympathetic nervous systems, which act independently to regulate your body's activities. The parasympathetic and sympathetic nervous systems allow harmony in your body functions to achieve a state of balance, called homeostasis, in your regular life.

- *The parasympathetic nervous system*: This system controls the body's response during rest. This is meant to save and maintain energy for functions such as digestion, lung control during normal breathing, and regulating the bladder when you are urinating.
- *The sympathetic nervous system*: The *fight*-or-*flight* response is regulated by the sympathetic nervous system. When your brain deems a situation dangerous, it prepares your body to face or altogether avoid it by moving away. The sympathetic nervous system activates the release of noradrenaline and epinephrine, which are hormones that work to increase the brain's vigilance, selective attention, and arousal. The sympathetic nervous system also allows increased blood flow to your skeletal muscles to facilitate greater oxygen uptake (Sherin & Nemeroff, 2011).

In cases such as PTSD, the sympathetic nervous system's response becomes extreme, such that your body may judge some experiences with intense terror or helplessness in anticipation of harm or intense body pain. The extent to which your body will react largely depends on the specific traumatic experiences you have encountered. The psychological trauma triggered by PTSD is characterized by rapid and vivid flashbacks of unpleasant thoughts and memories, causing irritability, confusion, dissociation, anger, and confusion, among other symptoms. These symptoms may cause a destabilized sympathetic nervous system due to constant arousal by the continuous negative triggers.

THE PHYSICAL MANIFESTATION OF TRAUMA: WHEN THE BODY SPEAKS

Trauma manifests in different ways depending on the exact experiences that you have gone through. These experiences are unique for every individual, such that trauma symptoms can vary significantly from one person to another. Traumatic experiences are unpleasant to the mind, and the body will also have an adverse physical reaction toward them. This is why it is common to experience symptoms such as body pain, muscle tension, tiredness, and headaches whenever you bring traumatic experiences to mind. When the thoughts of such experiences are so overwhelming, they can even disrupt your sleep patterns and eating habits. This has a cascading negative impact on your physical health since you won't be able to focus and do the normal things you would like.

Dr. Bessel van der Kolk underscored the impact of trauma on the physical body in his book *The Body Keeps the Score*. He outlines that when you encounter a traumatic experience, your muscles store the information about the experience through signals from the brain. He says this is because experiences and events have emotions attached to them. He also highlights that you can consciously wire new emotions and perspectives to particular events if you want to overcome the negative psychological impacts of traumatic experiences. These new feelings will override the traumatic memories each time you encounter experiences that trigger them (Z. Williams, 2021).

It is important to note that the body stores the physiological effects of traumatic events, even when the mind tries to suppress them. You may tell yourself you have healed, but the subconscious mind records everything. The rational mind tries to convince you that you are okay, but the physiological body says otherwise. You may realize a tendency to irrationally superimpose your traumatic experiences onto everything around you or to disconnect from the reality around you.

Dr. van der Kolk stresses that this is why therapy is extremely vital to effectively dealing with traumatic experiences. He further explains that no single therapy could be effective on its own. Instead, your unique experiences will require customized treatment based on how your body reacts to trauma and how it stores the stress in your muscles. Your particular treatment will also depend on your hormonal balance, which is different among individuals. Therefore, there is a need to incorporate pharmaceutical medication to address physical tension in your body, in addition to therapy, so that you facilitate overall recovery from trauma.

THE PSYCHOLOGICAL EFFECTS OF TRAUMA

The symptoms of trauma vary among individuals, usually linked to PTSD, the extent of which is dependent on the nature of the traumatic experiences. According to the U.S. Department of Veterans Affairs, the average likelihood of an American developing PTSD at some point in their life is 6%, with that of men being 4%. In comparison, that of women is 8% (National Center for PTSD, 2023).

More subtle and less obvious signs and symptoms of trauma may not be easily diagnosed and are usually because of people's different abilities to handle their experiences. Some people are better able to subdue the symptoms of trauma. Others may be more prone to showing the symptoms due to several factors, including their genetic disposition and the frequency and extent of the traumatic experiences. Some of the psychological impacts of trauma are outlined below:

- *Emotional effects*: Some of the emotions that are associated with traumatic events include guilt, shame, anger, fear, and sadness. You may be unable to identify these feelings when the trauma is severe, and you may exhibit them as a coping mechanism without realizing it. Emotional reactions vary significantly between people depending on their personal history of trauma and their ability to handle emotions.

- *Cognitive effects*: Traumatic experiences change your cognition, that is, how you see the world. For example, if you had a violent experience at night, you could begin to fear the event's recurrence due to the misplaced belief that all places are unsafe at night or that everyone you meet is probably out to attack you. Cognitive errors occur when one misinterprets or misjudges the outcome of a situation based on prior experiences that turned traumatic.
- *Somatization*: Somatization is the term used to describe conditions where the symptoms of psychological trauma manifest as physical ailments. This often occurs when you express emotional pain through physical engagement, such as going through a strenuous activity to cope with a trigger, until you start experiencing headaches. Over time, the headache becomes synonymous with the traumatic experience. Common physical symptoms of somatization include disorderly sleep patterns, constant headaches, cardiovascular problems, and dermatological issues.
- *Shortened projections of the future*: Trauma can cause you to limit your positive expectations for the future. You could become hopeless about the future with the false belief that you do not deserve a normal life or that your life could end at any moment.

- *Flashbacks, intrusive memories, and nightmares*: Traumatic events can cause random, uncontrollable flashbacks about the painful experiences that you endured. The mental recollection of these events is intrusive and may even disturb your sleep at night, causing you nightmares.
- *Numbing*: Numbing is a situation whereby you deliberately detach yourself from the memories of your traumatic experiences. With this practice, you go through the motions of your life without any responsiveness to the things that would ordinarily trigger you.

UNDERSTANDING TRIGGERS

A trigger reminds you of a traumatic event and provokes you to a specific response. Triggers often occur when your traumatic history flashes before your mind because of situations or images that cause you to relive the past experience. Recognizing and understanding triggers is an essential step in managing trauma responses. Therefore, let's have a look at the different types of triggers:

- *Internal triggers*: These are feelings you experience because of prior negative encounters that are similar to what you may be observing. For instance, if you got accidentally hit by a speeding car in the past, you may be triggered by any vehicle you see, even while watching it on television.

- *External triggers*: These encounters bring back flashes of traumatic experiences because of the senses of sight, touch, smell, hearing, and taste. For example, if you meet someone with a hairstyle similar to your abuser, you are more likely to be triggered and taken back to the traumatic experience.
- *Symptom triggers*: You encounter these triggers when you change a routine or activity in order to cope with something, and then the result provokes even greater symptoms. For example, let's suppose that you engage in binge eating to cope with a past traumatic experience. You may find that the negative thoughts of overeating and risking obesity may trigger other symptoms like depression.
- *Trauma triggers*: These are similar to external triggers but are usually more intense. For example, war veterans who constantly experience bomb blasts may be easily triggered by the detonation of explosives at a construction site.

Take some time to determine your triggers as you work toward healing. This is because being aware of your triggers and learning coping strategies can help you to manage the negative impact and reduce their distressing effects.

COPING WITH TRAUMA RESPONSES

Coping with trauma may appear difficult at first because of the mental weight it carries. If you experienced trauma for a more significant part of your childhood under different circumstances, many random things will likely trigger you in adulthood. In such cases, the strategy that may seem plausible to you may be to use avoidance as a coping mechanism. This can be helpful as an immediate coping strategy. However, avoidance often leads to isolation and depression. It is also impossible to avoid every situation that triggers you, especially if there are many. If this is the case with you, you may add some of the following strategies to help you:

Focusing on Your Five Senses (5-4-3-2-1 Method)

Allow yourself to be consciously aware of each of your five senses at any given time and focus on what they are individually experiencing. For example, you can consciously feel a cool breeze while breathing in slowly, looking at birds flying in the sky, smelling the beautiful scent of flowers, and chewing gum simultaneously. This brings you to the present moment and has a calming effect on your mind.

Breathing Slowly and Deeply

In this method, you consciously inhale air and keep it in for a while before exhaling it much slower than the rate at which you took it in. This activates your nervous system response, which is responsible for calming you down. You can set a rhythm to follow, for example, breathing in slowly for a count of three, holding the air in up to the fifth count, and then exhaling for a much longer time, like up to seven counts.

Sleeping Under a Heavy Blanket

Research shows that sleeping under a heavy blanket reduces stressful feelings, anxiety, and depression as it imitates a gentle hug (Lees, 2020). This subconsciously evokes emotions of feeling safe and wanted.

The "Window of Tolerance" Strategy

The imaginary *window of tolerance* represents the range of feelings you can control when exposed to your triggers. Outside this window are the emotions that you cannot comfortably contain. As your ability to control various emotions increases, so does the size of your window of tolerance. This method helps you stay in the present when you are triggered by focusing only on what you can manage while ignoring the rest.

Laughing

Laughing is therapeutic as it helps you reduce stress. Find a company that makes you laugh, or watch a funny movie to improve your mood.

Positive Thinking for Just 12 Seconds

New neuron connections in your mind take just about 12 seconds to form, according to Dr. Rick Hanson (Lees, 2020). Forming new neural connections relieves stress and soothes your emotions. You can do this by bringing a positive experience or thought to mind and focusing on it for just 12 seconds.

Validating Your Experience

Validating your experience means acknowledging your trauma, the pain it has caused you, and going through the emotions as they come. When you speak to a therapist, they validate your experience by actively listening, tolerating, reinstating what you just said, and showing that they take you seriously. With this method, you can gradually begin to stop blaming yourself for what you went through. It brings you to the present reality of your life, away from the trauma, and helps you gradually tame your fears until you realize they are no longer a living reality. This helps you heal much easier on your own without needing any medication.

This chapter has taken you through the changes in your body and its response to psychological trauma. The nervous system is responsible for your body's response to what you encounter. As you take steps to heal from the traumatic experiences that you have encountered, there are many strategies that you can implement on your own to help you cope. These include focusing on your five senses to stay in the present, taking deep slow breaths, and taking a few seconds to focus on positive thoughts. As you do these things, you will begin your journey to recovery, which is what the following chapter addresses.

3

JOURNEY TO RECOVERY—ONE STEP AT A TIME

Regardless of the extent to which you have been affected by trauma, healing is possible. However, the rate at which you can do so varies between individuals. This chapter will delve into the nitty-gritty of the essential steps you need to embark on your healing journey. We will emphasize the importance of patience, self-love, and a supportive environment in your endeavors to feel safe and rebuild the trust you used to have for yourself and others.

Some of the ideas we will highlight were practiced by celebrities like Oprah Winfrey, who had traumatic experiences during her childhood. At some point, Oprah said, "It's my teachers that saved me" (KVC Health Systems, 2021). This showed the positive impact that certain people had on Oprah's journey to recovery. Not only that,

Oprah is a great advocate for *self-love*, which enhances your self-esteem and the courage to deal with trauma.

Get ready to explore more effective and practical strategies that we will discuss in this chapter.

ACKNOWLEDGING YOUR TRAUMA: THE FIRST STEP TOWARD HEALING

The fact that trauma may bring hopelessness cannot be overstated. As a result, some people may feel stuck in that state, and this derails their healing process. On the contrary, your healing process can only begin when you acknowledge and accept what you went through. Considering that most trauma is associated with loss and love, you must realize that these two components are an inevitable part of life. Therefore, accepting the reality of life is a good starting point for your healing journey. Dr. Bessel van der Kolk once said that we "know what we know and feel what we feel" is what makes us better as life progresses (Mikelson, 2018). Therefore, you could picture what you went through as an essential part of your past that will make you stronger and better prepared for anything that comes your way.

Although acknowledging trauma is one of the vital steps for commencing your healing process, it is one of the most challenging things to do. One of the reasons why this happens is because some people may downplay their experiences. Such responses to trauma are usually instilled from childhood, especially if you grew up in a culture where mental health issues and emotional expression are stigmatized. As a result, you might feel that expressing yourself and accepting your past could make you appear weak.

Getting It Done

The *fight-or-flight* response is a survival mechanism. In both cases, action is involved, whether by facing your fears head-on or avoiding them in a way. When none of the two is done, you remain in that traumatizing state where you feel trapped, prevented, held down, and frozen. This state signifies that your usual response to frightful and unpleasant scenarios has been blocked. While in that state, your body continues to release stress hormones. This negatively affects the functionality of the prefrontal cortex of your brain, which is the part that deals with decision-making, learning and memory, complex planning, problem-solving, and executive functions. This literally means that your brain will be relatively offline. On the other hand, the emotional part of the brain, which is the amygdala and limbic system, will take control. Understanding these processes helps you better understand where you are right now so that you can take the right action to correct the situation.

Think of it this way. How do animals protect themselves from predators? They do this by either hiding and disguising themselves or by running away. Both responses have one thing in common, which is action. It takes courage for you to move on after significant incidences of betrayal and loss. In this case, you must recalibrate your nervous system so your prefrontal cortex returns to work. Mindfulness activities like yoga and meditation are effective in getting this done. You can also engage in breathing exercises that involve a deep connection with your body.

STEP 2: PATIENCE: UNDERSTANDING THE PACE OF HEALING

It's important to understand that healing from trauma isn't a race, so you don't need to compare yourself with other people. Similar to how people are affected by trauma to varying extents, their healing process also happens at different rates. Some studies have shown that timelines for recovering from traumatic experiences vary across individuals, mainly based on factors such as the type of trauma experienced, the individual's mental health history, and their coping mechanisms (Beidel et al., 2017). Therefore, you need to be patient with yourself when you address trauma, knowing that your healing is a process, not an event.

Sometimes, you will find your mind wandering into issues you thought you had dealt with. There is no need for you to hit yourself over that. Instead, exercise patience with yourself and continue to focus on your healing. You will also need to be patient with the people around you, especially those supporting you in your journey to recovery.

Here is an outline of some ideas that can help you to practice patience:

- *Don't strive for perfection; rather, concentrate on progress*: Questions like, "When will I start to see the real change?" are common among trauma survivors. It's because you can't wait to jump out of your situation. However, remember that each step of the way is progress. Therefore, don't focus much on the destination but on the journey itself.
- *Engage in techniques that reduce stress*: Stress can deter your progress, so you should do everything possible to lower it. Relaxation techniques such as meditation can help. You can also try exercising and getting enough sleep. Be sure to eat healthy foods, doing all you can to avoid saturated fats, added sugars, and processed foods.
- *Shower yourself with kindness* and direct it toward yourself. Say some kind words to yourself whenever you have the chance to. You can even schedule this activity. For example, you could tell yourself, *Robert, you are powerful every morning. I really cherish your courage*. You can create different kindness mantras to recite on different occasions. The more you say them, the more you believe them.

- *Try not to multitask*: Trauma may involve a combination of aspects, which include emotional breakdown, compromised trust, lost love, and increased fear. Tackling all the factors that define your trauma all at once can feel overwhelming, and this may take a toll on your patience. Try to address one thing at a time whenever possible. Doing this will also help you to notice the progress that you are making.
- *Embrace bad days*: When you experience a bad day, remind yourself that it is absolutely okay. Even those who are not dealing with trauma have bad days in their lives. Keep going!

STEP 3: SELF-LOVE AND SELF-COMPASSION: NURTURING YOUR EMOTIONAL WELL-BEING

Some researchers reported that practicing self-compassion is associated with lower levels of anxiety and depression (Werner et al., 2012). Both depression and anxiety are common in individuals who are victims of trauma. Humans are social beings who have an inner yearning for love and compassion. This is more so when you are in a state of being *broken*. While you may want others to support you, you must be your number one cheerleader. Channel some love and compassion toward yourself.

Dr. Kristin Neff, a pioneer in self-compassion research, highlighted that being kind to oneself significantly contributes to a state of well-being (Neff, n.d.). They define self-compassion as comparable to the love and kindness you give others. That particular feeling that you experience as part of empathy is what you now need to channel toward yourself. This time, get moved by your suffering, similar to what you would do when others are in trouble. Stop judging and blaming yourself, and embrace self-love. You can shower yourself with self-love and compassion in many ways. Let's explore some of them here.

Positive Self-Talk

You might know how negative self-talk can wear you down and make you feel worthless. Similarly, positive self-talk can do vice-versa. It uplifts your mood, boosts your courage, and arouses more positive emotions. Please note that your talk is a reflection of your pattern of thoughts. Therefore, you need to train your mind to dwell more in positivity, and this will improve how you talk about yourself and others.

Maya Angelou greatly believed in positive affirmations. She had a very traumatizing childhood, initially stemming from the abuse she suffered from her mother's boyfriend, who was later murdered. His death worsened Maya's mental state to the extent that she lost her voice for many years (R. Williams, 2021). It took encouragement from Maya's teacher for her to start speaking again. Reciting positive affirmations was one of the aspects that helped

Maya regain her confidence and redevelop a positive outlook on life. Maya won the "Women Who Move the Nation" award.

Here are some of the positive affirmations that you can use:

- *What I went through does not define me.*
- *It's okay to struggle, but I will get through it.*
- *Healing is not linear, so having bad days or weeks is okay.*
- *I celebrate the fact that I am a survivor!*
- *I will shower myself with love, patience, and compassion as I go through my healing process.*
- *I am not prone to harm.*
- *There is nothing wrong with my feelings. I am going through a healing process.*
- *I deserve to be loved, treated well, healed, feel better, and be in my best state of mind.*
- *I am enough and capable.*

Create and Maintain a Gratitude Journal

Research has proven that journaling is one of the effective techniques for dealing with trauma (Foy, 2020). It helps to counteract stress, which is one of the significant symptoms of trauma (Fekete & Deichert, 2022). Gratitude journaling is also reported to enhance cognitive function and the immune system, which puts you in a better position to fight trauma. You can also deal with emotions such as anger and anxiety using gratitude journaling.

When journaling, do not concentrate on issues such as spelling, but focus on the flow of your thoughts and ideas. Also, refrain from judging yourself in the process of writing.

Here is an outline of steps that can help you when creating your gratitude journal:

1. Identify a space where there are as few distractions as possible. Assume a comfortable position that you can hold for a relatively long time. It's okay to play some light music.
2. Take note of how you feel emotionally, psychologically, emotionally, and spiritually.
3. Sit still for a few minutes before you start writing anything. Meditate, allowing thoughts to freely pass through your mind without you judging them. Turn in on the *here-and-now* moment.
4. Start by writing anything that comes into your mind. This can include the frustrations and stress of the day.
5. Go on to list the things you are thankful for. Just write without judging yourself.
6. Assess how you are feeling in your body.

Treat Yourself

Treat yourself to things and activities that you love. Here, the goal is to create the inner joy that replaces the negative feelings associated with trauma at that particular time. You could try sports, cooking, baking, exercising, watching nature, or connecting with other people. Anything that gives inner satisfaction and fulfillment will do. When you identify what you want to do, schedule how often you will do it in a day, week, month, or year. Try to stick to your schedule even when you don't really feel like it.

STEP 4: LEVERAGING PERSONAL STRENGTHS: YOU ARE STRONGER THAN YOU BELIEVE

Some scientific studies have shown that strength-based interventions enhance a sense of well-being and reduce symptoms associated with depression (Proyer et al., 2015). Based on this reported information, identifying and utilizing your strengths is an essential part of your healing process. Your confidence and resilience are boosted as you get acquainted with your positive attributes. Your personal strengths can be anything, including being a good listener, excellent time management, persistence, creativity, critical thinking, and good problem-solving skills. Always remember that the trauma that you are going through does not define you. Rather, your abilities and strengths significantly contribute to who you are.

You might be wondering how best you can identify your strengths and abilities. Of course, there are some that you know already, but you might be surprised to note that there are some that you haven't been aware of. Use the following tips to determine your strengths and abilities:

- *Reflect on your past*: If you take an honest review of your past, you will realize that there are many times when you did well and triumphed. Such moments are partly attributed to the positive characteristics that define you. Identify such incidents and the strengths that are associated with them. Use those attributes to revamp yourself and tread toward your healing.
- *Ask others*: The people around you could be one of the best sources of information that you are looking for. If you ask your friends, family, and colleagues, you might discover some positive attributes you never knew you possessed. Approach many people while taking note of what they say. Review the responses later. The strengths and abilities that keep appearing in the findings are more likely to define you.
- *Assess what you do*: Take your notebook and write down what you love to do. Go further, determine why you love those activities, and derive your positive attributes from this information. For instance, you could write, "I love writing on topics encouraging others to believe in themselves. I

make sure I share the poems that I write so that they can reach as many people as possible." This would show that you are empathetic, caring, and resilient.

- *Use a personality test*: There are many personality tests that are available online. Personality tests are assessments that are based on a set of questions that are meant to determine who you are. The responses that you give define your strengths, abilities, and weaknesses. Some of the personality tests that you might want to try are the Myers–Briggs Type Indicator (MBTI), Big Five personality tests, Dominance, Influence, Steadiness, Conscientiousness (DiSC) assessment, Caliper Profile, and Minnesota Multiphasic Personality Inventory (MMPI).

STEP 5: CREATING A SAFE AND SUPPORTIVE ENVIRONMENT: A SANCTUARY FOR HEALING

Your healing is faster and more effective when you create a safe environment for the physical, emotional, and psychological aspects of your life. This environment includes the people whom you will allow into your circles. When supportive people surround you, you will feel safer, and this enhances your healing progress. The trauma-informed approach to dealing with the negative effects of unfortunate experiences emphasizes the need and importance of feeling safe (SAMHSA, n.d.). There are three ways you can create an environment that is safe and supportive of your recovery:

- *Create an inner haven for healing*: The first safe environment you should create is from within. You can't afford to be a threat to your own progress. Even though this might not be easy, encourage yourself to fight on. Recite positive affirmations, read encouraging stories of people who survived trauma, and watch motivating talk shows. Anything that will boost your confidence in dealing with the situation that you are in will suffice.
- *Surround yourself with the right people*: Identify positive people who can contribute to your progress and make efforts to form meaningful relationships with them. Your family and friends can give you the support that you need. You can also join support groups with people who have had similar experiences. This fosters encouragement among victims. Depending on what you are going through, counselors, therapists, and health professionals could be an important part of your connections. Avoid interactions that make you feel more hopeless and worthless. Once you notice such negative traits in your interactions, do everything possible to break away to guard the possibly little confidence you have left after the traumatic incident.

- *Create a positive physical space*: Create a peaceful physical environment that allows you to relax. If you think nature makes you feel calm and relaxed, adding some flowers to your spaces is a good idea. If you love art, incorporate such a space into your environment to trigger that inner joy that nurtures peace.

In this chapter, we highlighted the five steps you should take as you journey toward healing. These steps are acknowledging your trauma, fostering patience, being kind to yourself, leveraging personal strengths, and creating a safe and supportive environment. In the next chapter, we will discuss how you can use the support of the professionals who are relevant to your story.

4

GUIDED PATHWAYS—SEEKING PROFESSIONAL HEALTH FOR TRAUMA RECOVERY

Trauma may lead you to substance abuse as a coping mechanism. This makes it difficult for you to make an informed decision on your own regarding getting the help you need for your recovery, considering that you might not be in the right state of mind. Nuffield Trust (2023) reports that the number of people in America who contacted drugs and alcohol services between 2020 and 2021 during the COVID-19 pandemic and during the 2021–2022 period when the national lockdown was still in place were 275,896 and 289,215, respectively. The trust also established that there was a strong link between substance abuse and psychological trauma, as more than 70% of the people seeking help with addiction also had underlying mental issues that they required help on. These statistics show that once you have experienced psychological trauma, it is advisable for you to seek therapy early to reduce the risk of further deterioration, especially if substance abuse is involved. In this chapter, we will explore the importance of therapy in your recovery from trauma and the available options.

THE ROLE OF THERAPY IN TRAUMA RECOVERY

Your mind, body, and relationships make it necessary to seek professional help to deal with it effectively. As much as you may use some helpful personal strategies like practicing mindfulness to help you cope, getting professional help actually does more for you. Therapists have professional experience working with people who have faced similar traumas as yours. This improves their chances of diagnosing the proper treatment and therapy that enhances their recovery. Professional therapists also know how to engage with you in therapeutic dialogues, making it easier for you to open up on the things you need to, some of which you may not have been willing to share.

According to the American Psychologist Association (2022), therapy has been found to alleviate trauma symptoms in victims significantly. The healthy ways of coping implemented during professional therapy are usually established in line with your personal experiences and preferences, thereby increasing the sessions' likelihood of success. There are different approaches to professional therapy, and they are assigned depending on your individual traumatic experiences. The extent and nature of what you experienced and your personal preferences and needs determine the ideal therapy you will receive. Some of the professional therapeutic approaches are listed below:

Cognitive Processing Therapy

Cognitive processing therapy (CPT) is an effective behavioral therapy that is divided into 12 different sessions. This intervention is particularly useful in helping survivors adjust their perceptions regarding the triggers they associate with their traumatic experiences. The main focus of CPT is to encourage you as a survivor to mentally formulate your traumatic experiences in a new way that deliberately makes your triggers irrelevant to your present life. This therapy method has been shown to reduce PTSD symptoms arising from rape, child abuse, and war experiences, among others (American Psychological Association, 2017d).

Narrative Exposure Therapy

Narrative exposure therapy (NET) involves grouping a few people for up to 10 therapeutic sessions. This is because it focuses on traumatic experiences that affect groups of people or societies, such as cultural, social, or political injustices. NET is often effective and recommended for people seeking therapy on complex traumatic experiences, as with refugees. The persistent traumatic experiences that survivors of war and social injustices often go through may shape false perceptions in the victims concerning how their life is supposed to be. Therefore, the NET strategy is designed to help survivors overcome such thoughts by assisting them to reframe their mindset to new expectations supporting the life they want to live. PTSD survivors of war are recommended to undergo NET (American Psychological Association, 2017e).

Prolonged Exposure Therapy

Prolonged exposure (PE) is a cognitive behavioral therapy that teaches victims to confront their trauma-induced fears, situations, and emotions. It helps you to overcome the avoidance of triggers. Avoidance is a regressive habit that increases your fear of the memories of your traumatic experiences. This method assists you in realizing that your fears are only imaginary and not as big as your mind makes them appear. Therefore, you can ignore them without fearing them. PE therapy involves about 15 sessions, each spanning an average of one to two hours (American Psychological Association, 2017c).

Cognitive Behavioral Therapy

CBT helps you recognize the faults in your thinking, behavior, and problem-solving and how these affect your life and those around you. CBT enables you to formulate better ways of thinking, motivating you to behave better and developing confidence in your abilities. This way, you will learn to take responsibility for all your actions.

Consistent and regular therapy promotes healthier ways of handling your triggers, a critical step in your recovery from trauma. Over time, your traumatic symptoms will noticeably reduce, while your social engagement improves as you develop useful mechanisms for dealing with your experiences.

MEDICATION AS A SUPPORTIVE TOOL IN RECOVERY

In addition to therapy, medication can help to treat some of the symptoms of your traumatic experiences. Your mind is connected to your body in such a way that the state of your thoughts determines your physical health to a significant extent. Enduring trauma for a long time is associated with several underlying physical conditions. For example, chronic headaches can result from constantly allowing troubling thoughts through your head. Other physical conditions that often result from reliving your traumatic experiences include stomach disturbances and high blood pressure. You need to consult a medical professional to get prescribed medication to control these physical symptoms.

Some of these symptoms may be temporary, only triggered by your inability to cope with a trigger effectively. For example, exposure to a specific environment that triggers you may cause your heart rate to increase, thereby resulting in high blood pressure. Your therapist is more likely to assist you in finding helpful ways of dealing with your responses to the triggers without any medication. Suppose you continue to have the same adverse reaction to your triggers. In that case, your therapist will assign you to a medical professional who can prescribe the proper medication to lower your blood pressure.

Your therapist knows best when your physical condition can be subdued by regular therapy and when you need to get prescribed medication. Some medications are recommended for specific PTSD symptoms, some of which are highlighted in this section (National Institute for Health and Care Excellence, 2018):

- *Antipsychotics*: This type of drug reduces the frequency and extent of hallucinations, delusions, agitation, and inconsistent speech in people with PTSD. Antipsychotics should be taken under the careful supervision of a medical professional because some people living with PTSD may be unaware of their symptoms. As a result, they might not properly follow through the course of the medication.
- *Antidepressants*: The three drugs that are typically prescribed as antidepressants for different symptoms of PTSD are venlafaxine (Effexor), sertraline (Zoloft), and paroxetine (Paxil). These drugs work by stimulating the production of noradrenaline and serotonin, the hormones that

help to regulate your emotions and improve your mood. These neurotransmitter chemicals disrupt the pain signals sent to your body by the nerves.
- *Antiepileptics*: These drugs are prescribed for PTSD patients who are often attacked by epileptic seizures and convulsions. Antiepileptics reduce the severity, number, and duration of seizures. However, there is no cure for these symptoms of PTSD; they can only be regulated. As a victim, you should also be aware that some symptoms, like seizures, could persist even when taking antiepileptics.

Combining Medication With Therapy

Combining medication with therapy has been found to work effectively, according to a study conducted by Edna Foa, PhD, a psychologist based at the University of Pennsylvania, and Jonathan Davidson, MD, a psychiatrist at Duke University (Psychiatric Times, 2003). Their study concluded that even if PTSD was wrongly diagnosed as either anxiety or depression, the traumatic symptoms in the patient are more likely to reduce if they are treated with antidepressants. They also concluded that treating PTSD symptoms using combined medication and therapy is more effective at lower doses of the prescribed antidepressants.

The U.S. Food and Drug Administration recommended antidepressants like paroxetine and sertraline for treating

PTSD symptoms between 1999 and 2001. The ideal condition for treatment to work independently without medication must continue to be taken relatively longer, even though combining the two produces the best outcome (Psychiatric Times, 2003). According to Foa, PE therapy is likely to work better when combined with medication compared to other therapy methods.

Medication as Treatment, Not a Cure

Taking medication for psychological issues provides instant relief, which can help to regulate your behavior more rationally. You should, however, realize that medication is not a cure for underlying psychological issues. It only helps you to manage them better.

If you are given a prescription for medication by a health professional, they still need to monitor you to observe the side effects regularly. In some cases, though rare, your body may negatively react to certain medications that may trigger you and cause side effects. This is known as medication trauma or complexity and could worsen your psychological condition (Center for Health Care Strategies, 2018). However, this condition has very little likelihood of ever happening to you, although you would still need your professional caregiver to strictly monitor how your body responds to medication. Complications can be avoided if medication is quickly stopped in cases of medication complexity.

THE SEARCH FOR THE RIGHT THERAPIST

Your recovery will likely be quicker and more bearable if you engage with a therapist who understands you personally. Therapists are trained professionals, often with vast experience in dealing with patients with varying psychological conditions. However, for therapy to be effective, a comfortable relationship between you and your therapist before you can begin your sessions is of paramount importance.

Effective therapy requires you to open up and reveal intimate details about your life. The ability to do so depends mainly on the close communication and engagement you have with your therapist. As such, a personal connection between you and your therapist is vital. You cannot force a good therapeutic relationship, and the things you have in common with your therapist should come naturally.

If you begin your therapy sessions and find that you are not getting along with your therapist, changing your therapist on time is advisable. Here are a few things that you can do to ensure that you find a therapist who matches the treatment you need:

- *Familiarity and experience in dealing with your concerns*: Find a therapist with experience in handling psychological issues similar to yours. Such a therapist is more likely to designate the right approach toward recovery that suits you.

You are different from everyone else, and you will need a customized therapy approach to suit your needs. This is more likely to happen if you get a therapist who has worked with issues similar to yours.

- *The number of years that they have been in the practice*: If your therapist has more years of experience, it improves their chances of helping you to recover successfully. More experience means a greater variety of approaches to help victims recover.
- *The fees they charge for their service*: This is a factor you should consider before engaging with the therapist. Therapy sessions need to be conducted according to the schedule that is prepared for you. Once you begin the sessions, continuity is crucial for your progress and recovery. If you cannot meet the total cost for all the sessions up to completion, it is wise to find another therapist you can afford before you begin the sessions.

The abovementioned factors will help you narrow down your options for the right therapist. However, some other things need your discretion without you having to engage with the therapist to determine if they will suit you. Considering these factors should help you to make the final decision on the right therapist to engage:

- *How do you feel around the therapist?* Do you feel genuinely engaged and comfortable sharing your personal life with them, or do they feel distant and disconnected from you? Your recovery is psychological, meaning your thoughts and feelings must be maintained in their best state. Anything that does not make you feel your best should immediately be disregarded so that you can adequately recover.
- *How does their workspace look?* Aesthetics are essential for your recovery. What you see will affect what you think and how you feel. The environment should feel comfortable and secure.
- *Do you feel at ease with the therapist?* Your therapist should make you feel relaxed and at ease with sharing your stories. If they appear judgmental and make you question yourself in any regard, you need to disengage from them and look for another.
- *Do they interrupt you as you talk or allow you to express yourself fully?* This is an important consideration because therapy is based on fully expressing yourself so that your concerns can be understood entirely. Your diagnosis and recommended therapy for recovery will depend on how well your psychological needs have been understood.
- *Do they validate your concerns?* Your therapist needs to validate everything you say and how you

express yourself. Even if you express yourself under the influence of a trigger, everything you say must be considered valid. This will help them to diagnose the ideal therapy sessions for you.
- *Are they on time, and do they conduct the sessions to meet the intended purpose?* You should assess whether your therapist values your time. You paid for their service, so you must get priority whenever it is time for your sessions. They should not engage with anything or anyone else during your sessions. They also need to align your therapy sessions to help you recover and not mix that with irrelevant issues that do not directly concern you.

Finding a suitable therapist to meet your personal needs takes time, but do everything in your power to get one. Mental health institutions are more likely to have a vast catalog of recommended therapists who can help you. You can then apply the different approaches outlined in this section to narrow down your choices to the ones that suit your preferences. The American Psychological Association (2017d) also has various catalogs for professional therapists that you can choose from.

The best pathways toward your psychological recovery are outlined in this chapter, with further recommendations on how to explore them. Therapy is recommended for your recovery from trauma, especially if you have been diagnosed with PTSD. Therapy sessions are highly personal, and you can customize them based on the environment, personality, and style of the therapist that you prefer. The chapter has also given you recommended steps that you can take to ensure that you get a therapist who meets your expectations.

As you undergo therapy, you may also receive it in combination with medication to provide quicker recovery. Once you get the right therapist and go through the ideal sessions, you will naturally build resilience and become ready to bounce back. Steps to do so effectively are covered in the next chapter.

5

BOUNCING BACK—THE POWER OF ADAPTABILITY

Trauma can appear like a new norm, especially if you experience its long-term effects. As a result, breaking from the hold of the new patterns associated with trauma may require a great sense of adaptability, which comes through resilience.

Demi Lovato, who had her first experience with cocaine at the age of 27, experienced the power of adaptability as she worked toward her recovery from substance abuse (Porreca, 2021). Lovato's addiction was so high to the extent that she tried to smuggle drugs onto an airplane due to the fear that she wouldn't be able to go for one and a half hours without them. It took a fatal overdose that resulted from mixing Xanax and cocaine for Lovato to realize that she needed to make efforts to break away from drug addiction. She gathered the courage to seek help, which helped her build the resilience she needed to bounce back gradually. She is making efforts to adapt to a relatively new way of life that does not involve drugs.

Similarly, you have what it takes to attain and maintain a new norm that is void of fear, anxiety, and depression, regardless of what you went through. In this chapter, we unleash the nature of resilience and how you can implement the strategies to foster it. This will assist you in navigating life's challenges more effectively and grow from any form of trauma.

THE NATURE OF RESILIENCE: TURNING ADVERSITY INTO STRENGTH

The term *resilience* only gains a valid meaning when adversities or obstacles to progress are involved. This means that you can only be resilient if you face difficulties from which you have to bounce back. Resilience is not about avoiding difficulties but learning to thrive amid them. Instead of viewing challenges as impassable obstacles, resilient people see them as opportunities for learning, improvement, and ultimate victory.

Thomas Edison famously made 1,000 unsuccessful attempts at inventing the light bulb. During an interview, Edison was asked, "How did it feel to fail 1,000 times?" He responded, "I didn't fail 1,000 times. The light bulb was an invention with 1,000 steps" (Watkins, 2019).

Who Can Be Resilient?

Everyone has equal chances of developing resilience. Resilience is not a rare trait only in certain extraordinary people. This is because resilience can be described as a set of thoughts, behaviors, and actions that one can learn and develop over time. This definition alone makes resilience open to anyone.

Think of J. K. Rowling, the author of *Harry Potter*. Rowling was a single mother who survived on welfare. She had to deal with many setbacks before her book could be published. Twelve publishers rejected the draft for her book. You see, Rowling had the choice to stop and assume that publishing her book was an impossible attempt. The ability to deal with the frustration of getting rejected many times gave her the courage to resubmit her book for the 13th time. Surprisingly, there laid her breakthrough to becoming one of the most famous authors ever. Rowling displayed resilience when she was not recognized and had nothing much, especially financially. This further emphasizes the fact that anyone can be resilient, and that includes you.

BUILDING RESILIENCE: PRACTICAL STEPS TO FOSTER GROWTH

There is no *one-size-fits-all* method for developing resilience. This fact can be attributed to the differences in the factors that characterize each traumatic experience. In this section, we will look at some ideas that can help you foster resilience. You can customize the outlined nuggets to match your situation.

Reframe Your Perspective

Sometimes, it takes changing your perspective to give room for resilience. Choose to see opportunities in your adversities rather than to see them as the end of the road. For instance, you may choose not to view losing your job as a disaster but as an opportunity to explore other money-making ventures.

If you wonder if this works, think of icons like Walt Disney. You probably admire what he achieved, especially after he became a co-founder of Disney Brothers Cartoon Studio. However, did you know that Disney was fired from his job before he started trying to set up a business of his own? If he had continued to cry over his lost job, he wouldn't have probably won the accolades that he had and the fame that came with them.

Disney is not the only one who turned getting fired into an opportunity for more tremendous success. People like Oprah Winfrey, Thomas Edison, Mark Cuban, Madonna, and many more have done the same. So what if your adversities are just a way to force you to look the other way and start authoring your success?

Create a Strong Support Network

Creating and sustaining good relationships with other people significantly contributes to resilience. Interactions with others give you what is called social resilience. This is the strength you feel, mainly based on the feeling that you have the support of the people.

Let's suppose that you are walking in a scary environment. You are more likely to feel scared when alone than when walking with a group. Interestingly, social resilience also enhances your personal inner strength. You can think of this personal resilience as *borrowed* from others. Get the right people into your circles and gain the social resilience that will make you confident.

When you have supportive connections, whether inside or outside your family, you foster a sense of belonging. Good connections also enhance your self-worth and provide a safety net when tackling difficulties (Theisen, 2021).

Here are some ideas on how you can nurture meaningful and relevant relationships:

- Accommodate your family and friends as part of the support system
- Join groups that align with your hobbies and passions.
- Sign up for Meetup, which is a platform where you connect and interact with people who have interests that are similar to yours.

You can attend conferences that address topics that you are interested in. For example, if you are an academic, why not register for the upcoming conferences in your niche? If you are in business, many events are advertised. Make time to register and attend one or more of those. You never know who you will meet there.

Engage in Regular Self-Care

Considering that resilience is often built over time, taking good care of yourself is one of the effective ways to foster it. One study revealed a positive correlation between resilience and self-care in patients with chronic illnesses (Jin et al., 2022). These findings also apply to any situation that requires resilience for one to conquer.

Results from another study also emphasized that self-care activities could be regarded as mediators between resilience and the quality of your life (Abdollahi et al., 2022). This means that self-care endeavors contribute toward resilience, improving your life's overall quality.

There is a lot that you can do in a bid to promote self-care, and the following are not exempted:

- Engage in physical exercises such as swimming, jogging, stretching, and cycling.
- Incorporate mental exercises like puzzles.
- Eat a balanced diet with energy-boosting foods such as plant-based ones.
- Drink a lot of water to keep your body hydrated.

- Practice relaxation techniques such as meditation.
- Get some rest, whether by taking a break from regular activities or getting adequate sleep.
- Utilize technology through apps like Calm, which offers guided meditation and stories that help you relax and remain calm.

Exercising, resting, and eating well help to boost your physical and mental energy. This will see your overall resilience improve. Relaxation also reduces stress, regret, anxiety, and associated depression. This improved mental wellness contributes to more resilience.

RESILIENCE IN ACTION: REAL-LIFE EXAMPLES

The evidence of resilience is not far-fetched. It is clearly seen in people we see physically and online. Sometimes, we read about stories that reflect remarkable resilience, not really with the aim of learning. In this section, we will reflect on some of the stories worth noting, with a more conscious motive to derive meaningful lessons about resilience.

Oprah Winfrey

Oprah Winfrey had her own fair share of the trauma that poverty can bring. She was sexually abused at a tender age and had no one to stand up for her. At one point, Winfrey experienced teenage pregnancy as a result of the sexual abuse that she was enduring. Upon giving birth to her child, the baby did not live long. All these were adversities that Winfrey had to bear.

As an adult, Winfrey struggled through various incidents that threatened her emotional stability. One such incident was when she was fired from her job. Despite what she had been through, Winfrey maintained her determination and perseverance against all odds. Today, she is one of the most admired self-made billionaires, and it's worth noting that she is a woman. You can also defy the odds and make it!

Walt Disney

We once mentioned Walt Disney in this chapter. However, one of the things that we didn't clarify was the fact that Disney tried to form other businesses before the successful Disneyland. The businesses were unsuccessful, a situation that could render him hopeless. However, Disney continued to soldier on, creating a legacy that still lives, even after he died. It is also worth mentioning that Disney was fired for "lacking creativity." Interestingly, his innovations were a sure sign that he was creative after all!

You can choose whether to allow trauma to define your destiny or not. Build resilience and become what no one ever thought you could be.

Michael Jordan

You might have heard of Michael Jordan, the famous basketball player who became a role model for many upcoming players. While Jordan's success seemed obvious, you might be surprised to hear that he had his own share of failures that would have derailed him if he had not been resilient.

During his high school years, Jordan was dropped from the team. His coaches at that time described him as a slacker. Despite all this, Jordan maintained his focus and trained even more. Such resilience offered him an opportunity as a member of great teams such as the Tar Heels and Chicago Bulls. In his own words, Jordan (n.d.) says,

I've missed more than 9,000 shots in my career. I've lost almost 300 games. Twenty-six times, I've been trusted to take the game-winning shot and missed. I've failed over and over and over again in my life. And that is why I succeed.

This quote is enough to tell you that failure is part of the learning process on your way to success. No matter how often you struggle with triggers and trauma symptoms, you will still be a victor if you foster resilience.

Colonel Harland Sanders

Colonel Harland Sanders was a chicken enthusiast with his own recipe for making chicken. He tried to sell his recipe to many restaurants, yet they dismissed him. By many, we are referring to more than 1,000 restaurants. That number is too big for a person to keep trying unless they are *resilient*. Well, the colonel fell under the bracket of the resilient. Kentucky Fried Chicken, popularly known as the KFC, is one of the highly competitive recipes on the market. Trying once or twice isn't enough. Don't get tired of making efforts to escape the negative effects of trauma.

Sylvester Stallone

Sylvester Stallone is a successful movie star, writer, director, and painter. However, Stallone did not become successful overnight. He had to go through various hurdles before making it in his career. Stallone faced a lot of discouragement from childhood, even for how he talked. He desired to be a movie star. Since he couldn't afford a proper gym, he started by lifting cinder blocks suspended from a broom. He tried to look for opportunities to be an actor but to no avail. His condition was so destructive to the extent that he had to sell his dog for only $25.00. There were times when Stallone was homeless and had to sleep at a bus station.

Even after all this, Stallone did not give up on his dreams. Stallone then wrote a script for Rocky, and he wanted to be the star in the movie. His offer was completely denied, so he took a role far less than what he wanted. However, this was his first breakthrough that would allow him to showcase his talent. The film succeeded, and Stallone's determination kept pushing him upward in the film industry. Imagine if Stallone had not been resilient; he would probably have remained homeless and hopeless. Instead, he defied all odds and still made it. You are no different. Just choose to be resilient, escape trauma, and reclaim your position as a successful person.

Everyday Heroes

In addition to the celebrities, some everyday heroes exemplify resilience in overcoming trauma. Consider a local community leader who spearheaded a neighborhood revitalization project after surviving a devastating hurricane. Their story serves as a testament to the power of resilience in turning adversity into positive change. Another good example is a teacher who, after experiencing a violent crime, started a self-defense class to empower others in her community. Her story underscores the potential of resilience in transforming personal trauma into communal empowerment. What about the parents who lost their child to a drunken driver and then decided to form a movement that supports other guardians who would have been affected by similar incidents?

Resilience is indispensable if you want to make it out of trauma. This is because recovery from trauma may stretch for longer, and it is easier to give up when adversities span through bigger time frames. Under such circumstances, resilience is what will keep you standing.

In this chapter, we explored various aspects of resilience and even gave you real-life examples of people who applied the power of resilience and made it in life. People like Oprah Winfrey, Walt Disney, and Sylvester Stallone are known for their unwavering resilience. In Chapter 6, we will explore how you can harness the power hidden within you as you deal with trauma.

Make a Difference with Your Review
Unlock the Power of Healing

> *"The greatest gift you can give is a portion of yourself." - Ralph Waldo Emerson*

Did you know that helping others can bring joy and meaning to your own life? It's true! When we help others, especially without expecting anything in return, we often feel happier and more fulfilled.

So, I have a special request for you...

Would you be willing to help someone who has experienced something difficult, even if you don't get any recognition for it?

You might be wondering, "Who is this person?" They could be a lot like you. They might have faced hard times and are looking for ways to heal and grow. They need guidance, just like you may have needed at one point.

Our goal is to make understanding and overcoming trauma accessible to everyone. Everything I do is driven by this mission. To achieve this, we need to reach as many people as possible.

That's where you come in. Most people choose books based on their covers and what others say about them. So, here's my request on behalf of someone struggling with trauma, who you've never met:

Please help them by leaving a review of this book.

Your review doesn't cost a thing and takes less than a minute, but it could change someone's life forever. Your words might help…

…another person find hope in their healing journey.

…someone discover ways to overcome their challenges.

…an individual find peace and emotional well-being.

…a reader find support and understanding in their path to recovery.

…another soul to start a new chapter in their life.

To feel great and truly make a difference, all you need to do is…take less than a minute to…

leave a review.

Just scan the QR code below to share your thoughts:

[Click here to leave your review on Amazon.](#)

If the idea of helping someone you've never seen makes you feel good, then you're exactly the kind of person I admire. Welcome to the club. You're one of us.

I'm even more excited to help you find understanding and healing in ways you never imagined. You're going to appreciate the insights and strategies coming up in the next chapters.

Thank you from the depth of my heart. Now, let's continue on our journey together.

Your biggest fan, Salina Crespin

PS - Fun fact: When you offer something valuable to someone else, it increases your value to them. If you think this book can help another person on their healing journey, why not share it with them?

6

EMPOWERMENT FROM WITHIN—HARNESSING YOUR INNER STRENGTH

Life presents us with various challenges, big and small, and it is easy to feel overwhelmed or reliant on external sources of motivation. However, true empowerment comes from recognizing the incredible potential that resides within ourselves. Harnessing your inner strength involves accessing your *well* of power, resilience, and determination. It is a journey of self-discovery, self-awareness, and self-actualization. If you unleash your inner strength, you will live a lifestyle that reflects the values, aspirations, and visions you want.

This chapter will explore the transformative journey of discovering and harnessing your inner strength. We will delve into the process of self-discovery and introspection to uncover your authentic self. Additionally, we will examine the role of resilience and determination in empowering you to navigate adversity and find meaning amid challenges.

UNEARTHING YOUR INNER STRENGTH: THE HIDDEN POWER WITHIN

Inner strength is a dynamic combination of mental resilience, emotional intelligence, and personal determination. It is not just about physical prowess but also about having the mental and emotional fortitude to face challenges, stay grounded, and persevere. Developing these aspects of yourself empowers you to navigate life's ups and downs with grace and courage.

According to a study published in the Journal of Happiness Studies, researchers found that people who see themselves as emotionally strong are more likely to use positive coping strategies when faced with challenges (Agnew, 2017).

A quote by Zig Ziglar, a renowned author and motivational speaker, hits the nail on the head. He said, "It's your attitude, not your aptitude, that will determine your altitude" (University of Pacific, 2022). Based on this quote, it is not just about what you are naturally capable of or your skills and abilities. It is also about how you approach and navigate life's challenges. Your attitude, mindset, and mental resilience significantly determine how high you can soar, regardless of your obstacles.

Personal determination is a key factor in the recovery process. One study published in 2015 reported that individuals with high levels of determination are more likely to adhere to healthy behaviors that aid in trauma recovery (Center for Substance Abuse Treatment, 2014). This means a strong personal drive and commitment can significantly impact the healing journey. When you possess personal determination, the probability of staying consistent with positive health behaviors supporting your recovery is relatively high. This could involve following a treatment plan, exercising regularly, practicing self-care, and making healthy lifestyle choices.

Discovering Your Inner Strength Through Introspection and Self-Reflection

Discovering your inner strength is all about taking the time to look within and reflect on yourself. Introspection is looking inward to assess your thoughts, emotions, and experiences. It requires pausing, disconnecting from external distractions, and tuning in to your inner world. Through introspection, you gain a deeper understanding of your beliefs and motivations.

Self-reflection, on the other hand, is the act of contemplating your experiences, actions, and choices. It involves examining your past behaviors, considering their impact, and identifying patterns or areas for growth. Self-reflection is like hitting the pause button and thinking about your actions, choices, and experiences. It is about looking back and asking yourself, *Why did I react that way?* Or, *What can I learn from this situation?* It is a way to gain insights about yourself and grow from them. Both introspection and self-reflection provide opportunities for self-awareness. They allow you to tune into your emotions, desires, and aspirations.

There are also several effective ways to tap into your inner strength. Here are some ideas:

- *Keep a personal journal*: As the University of Rochester Medical Center recommended, one suggestion is to keep a personal journal. It is a simple but powerful method that can help you gain a deeper understanding of your thoughts and feelings. If you write things down, you can explore your experiences, reflect on your challenges, and gradually uncover your inner strength.
- *Engage in mindfulness activities*: Another fantastic practice that can enhance self-awareness and help you recognize your inner strength is mindfulness. There is a great app called Insight Timer that promotes mindfulness practices. It offers guided meditations, breathing exercises, and even courses on self-discovery. Dedicating some time each day to mindfulness can cultivate a greater sense of presence and connect with the inner reservoir of strength within you.

- *Heed constructive feedback*: Getting constructive feedback from people you trust is also powerful. It turns out that feedback can be a valuable alternative for discovering your strengths and nurturing your inner power. An article in the Harvard Business Review highlights the significant role of feedback in personal growth (Alkan et al., 2016). When you receive feedback from trusted individuals, it provides a fresh perspective on your abilities and qualities. It helps you gain insights into areas where you excel and need further development. This feedback acts as a mirror that reflects your unique strengths and talents that may be hidden or unrecognized.

Harnessing Your Inner Strength Using Consistent Practice and Patience

There are a few key things to remember when harnessing your inner strength. According to the American Psychological Association, one effective approach is regularly practicing resilience-building exercises (American Psychological Association, 2020). Consistently engaging in these exercises can tap into your inner reservoir of strength and cultivate a mindset that helps you navigate challenges with greater resilience.

You should also have patience. Personal transformation and growth may take time to materialize. The renowned psychologist Dr. Robert Brooks emphasizes the significance of having patience along the journey. You should understand that changes do not happen overnight, so you should be patient with yourself as you work toward unleashing your inner strength.

Celebrating small victories can be immensely helpful. The Mayo Clinic suggests acknowledging and celebrating even the smallest achievements can motivate you, boosting your inner strength. Recognizing and appreciating your progress builds momentum and maintains a positive mindset that propels you forward.

INNER STRENGTH IN ACTION: EMPOWERING YOUR RECOVERY

Leveraging your inner strength involves taking proactive steps and actively participating in your recovery process. This could mean seeking professional help, implementing self-care habits, and making conscious choices that propel you forward.

Embracing an active role in your recovery brings a sense of progress and accomplishment. Even small steps can make a difference and reinforce your inner resolve. Each choice and goal you set contributes to a sense of empowerment, strengthening your belief in your capabilities. Additionally, prioritizing self-care and well-being is vital. Taking care of yourself equips you with the inner resources that help you to face challenges with determination and strength.

When you have strong personal determination, overcoming obstacles and staying committed to your recovery journey becomes easier. It is that unwavering belief in yourself that propels you forward. Whether following a treatment plan, implementing healthy habits, or making positive changes, personal determination helps you stay on course, even when faced with setbacks or difficult moments.

Inner Strength Can Fuel Resilience

When you are recovering from trauma, harnessing your inner strength can make a world of difference. It is akin to tapping into a deep well of personal resources that empower you to bounce back from setbacks and keep moving forward. The American Psychological Association backs this up, emphasizing the powerful connection between inner strength and resilience.

A strong inner self can foster resilience in the face of trauma. That inner reserve of strength, courage, and determination helps you weather the storm and rise above difficult circumstances. When you possess inner strength, you develop a resilient mindset that enables you to adapt, cope, and recover from your challenges.

The work of Dr. Martin Seligman on learned optimism can be a real game-changer when it comes to building resilience and strengthening your inner strength (Moore, 2019). Dr. Seligman's research highlights the power of cultivating an optimistic mindset and its impact on your ability to bounce back from setbacks. If you learn to view challenges as temporary and manageable, you can develop a resilient outlook that helps you to persevere through tough times.

Inner Strength Enhances Self-Efficiency and Boosts Confidence

When you tap into your inner strength, the extent to which you believe in yourself grows, and your confidence in handling trauma-related challenges gets a powerful boost. This idea aligns with what Albert Bandura, a renowned psychologist, refers to as the "self-efficacy theory" (Moore, 2016). According to Bandura, believing in your abilities to succeed is crucial in how you approach goals, tasks, and challenges. A strong sense of inner strength fuels your self-efficacy, which is your belief in your capability to handle and overcome difficult situations.

When you harness your inner strength, you feel more capable of taking on the challenges of trauma recovery. This newfound confidence empowers you to face challenges with determination and resilience. Building inner strength requires some time, but when you continue to nurture and tap into that inner well of strength, you will find that your self-efficacy and confidence in handling trauma-related challenges will keep growing.

Self-efficacy is a powerful factor that can boost your confidence in managing trauma-related symptoms, making the recovery process less overwhelming. One study suggests self-efficacy can predict recovery outcomes in individuals with PTSD (Luszczynska et al., 2009). This finding highlights just how vital self-efficacy is in the journey of healing from trauma.

MAINTAINING YOUR INNER STRENGTH: AN ONGOING COMMITMENT

Keeping your inner strength intact is an ongoing journey that involves a steadfast commitment to personal growth and self-improvement. It's about making yourself a priority and actively seeking opportunities to better yourself. This could mean learning new skills, exploring therapy or counseling to work through any challenges, or engaging in activities that make you happy. The key is to embrace a mindset of continuous learning and development so you can navigate life's ups and downs with resilience and a sense of empowerment.

Self-reflection has a significant role in maintaining inner strength. Taking the time to understand yourself and your needs allows you to engage in good choices and adapt to life's challenges. Regular self-reflection helps you identify areas for growth, set meaningful goals, and make adjustments as needed.

According to the Greater Good Science Center, self-reflection is an effective way to stay connected with your inner strength (Greater Good Science Center, 2019). It's like taking a pause and looking inward to gain a deeper understanding of yourself and your experiences. By setting aside time for self-reflection through whatever means, like journaling, meditating, or quiet contemplation, you create space to process your thoughts and emotions, identify patterns, and gain insights into your inner world. This process can help you recognize your strengths, values, and areas for growth, ultimately fostering a stronger connection with your inner strength.

As Dr. Carol Dweck proposed, Embracing a growth mindset is vital for nurturing inner strength (Sharma, 2023). It involves believing in the potential for personal development through effort, learning, and resilience. Instead of perceiving challenges as obstacles, a growth mindset views them as opportunities to develop and improve. With a growth mindset, you cultivate curiosity, embrace discomfort, and persist in facing setbacks. This mindset enables you to see setbacks as temporary hurdles and fuels your determination to keep striving, learning, and evolving. Adopting a growth mindset unlocks the power to expand your capabilities and continuously tap into your inner strength. This mindset fosters a lifelong learning and self-improvement journey, empowering you to navigate life's challenges with resilience and a greater sense of possibility.

Establishing a Support Network Can Bolster Your Inner Strength

Did you know that having a strong support system can boost your resilience? According to a study published in the Journal of Traumatic Stress, researchers found that social support plays a significant role in enhancing resilience and strengthening your inner self (Southwick et al., 2011). When you have friends, family, or even a community who support you, this indirectly helps you build inner strength. It is tantamount to having a safety net that catches you when you stumble, reminding you that you are not alone as you face challenges. These connections and relationships provide comfort, encouragement, and a reminder of your strength. The study highlights the importance of nurturing social connections and seeking support from others. It is not just about having someone to vent to but having individuals who truly care about your well-being and those who can offer guidance and understanding when you need it most.

Being part of a community or joining support groups can be beneficial for reinforcing your inner strength. Take, for example, the Mental Health America website. They have these amazing support groups that cater to different mental health needs. When you join such groups, you connect with people who understand what you are going through. Being part of a community gives you a sense of belonging. You realize that you are not alone in your struggles. You meet with others who have faced similar challenges and are there to listen and share their own experiences. Knowing that you have people who understand and accept you can be incredibly comforting.

In support groups, you can freely express yourself without fearing judgment. Knowing that you are in a safe space, you can talk about your feelings, fears, and triumphs. This kind of acceptance and validation can boost your confidence and reinforce your inner strength. Moreover, being part of these groups exposes you to different perspectives and valuable resources. You can learn from others, gain new insights, and discover helpful tools and strategies for managing your mental health. It is tantamount to having a wealth of knowledge and support right at your fingertips.

Setbacks Are "Only" a Part of Your Journey

Setbacks are just a natural part of your journey through life. They happen to everyone, and they do not mean it is the end of the road for you. It is ideal to remember that experiencing setbacks does not make you any less strong. These challenging moments can be incredible opportunities for growth and learning. Think of setbacks as these unexpected teachers that show up on your journey. They might not be the most pleasant guests, but they do have some valuable lessons to offer. When life throws challenges your way and setbacks seem to pop up left and right, it is easy to feel discouraged. Nevertheless, you should know that setbacks hold the keys to unlocking your resilience and inner strength.

Setbacks push you to dig deep and tap into your inner resources, helping you discover your capabilities. In those moments, you can pause, reflect, and learn. They expose areas where you can improve, strategies that may need some tweaking, or even perspectives that need to be shifted entirely.

Have you ever heard of Les Brown? He is a motivational speaker who knows how to inspire. He has this excellent quote that hits home: "You are more than you think" (Brown, 2021). It's a simple yet powerful statement that reminds us that our inner strength is always there, no matter our obstacles. Sometimes, when life throws challenges, you might doubt yourself and question whether you have what it takes to overcome them. However, Les Brown provides a quote that is a powerful reminder that your strength runs deeper than you realize.

As we conclude Chapter 6, it is clear that harnessing your inner strength is crucial when facing adversity and trauma. If you tap into your innate resilience and personal resources, you empower yourself to navigate the recovery process more effectively and meaningfully. Now, let us dive into Chapter 7, where we will tackle another essential aspect of healing: rebuilding trust in relationships after trauma. We will explore how trauma impacts our connections with others and provide practical strategies to navigate these challenges.

7

REBUILDING BRIDGES

Building and maintaining personal relationships is very important for your mental well-being. When your mental state is unstable, how you relate with those around you may be negatively affected. Psychological trauma affects how you see the people around you by compromising your judgment. When your judgment is affected, you may fail to recognize why people do what they do, increasing the probability of responding inappropriately. Inappropriate behavior negatively affects your relationships as more people may no longer be comfortable with being around you in fear of how you may react to them.

According to a Child Trends report, up to 46% of American children have been subjected to childhood trauma in some way (Scribner, 2014). Childhood trauma negatively affects your relationships with other people as you grow older. This is because the parts of the brain affected by trauma still develop during childhood, so the experiences you encounter are quickly ingrained in the mind. These experiences may affect you for life if you don't receive therapy.

The famous Hollywood actor Tyler Perry suffered traumatic abuse as a child. He was physically abused by his father and sexually traumatized by three adult men. Perry grew up harboring his traumatic recollections because he thought no one would understand him if he shared them. This built up anger within him as he approached his 20s, which affected most of his relationships with those around him (Fernández & Green, 2019). This chapter addresses how trauma affects your relationships and the steps you can take to heal and rebuild damaged relationships.

THE IMPACT OF TRAUMA ON PERSONAL RELATIONSHIPS

Trauma affects how you see the world and influences how you relate to people. The negative influence of trauma is that it destroys your sense of judgment, making you overreact even to the slightest provocation. Here are some of the psychological impacts that are related to trauma:

- *You project the traumatic experiences you encountered onto everyone else*: Everyone deserves a chance to be considered for who they are and not for what you project onto them. Not everyone is out to manipulate you. The prejudice that may develop in your mind due to trauma may make it difficult for people to relate with you.

- *Fear of forming close relationships with anyone*: If your traumatic experiences were severe, you may be afraid of forming close relationships with people. You may feel that interacting with people makes you more vulnerable to unpleasant experiences.
- *Social uneasiness*: Childhood trauma can make you feel guilty, ashamed of yourself, and unworthy, such that you may end up withdrawing and isolating yourself from people. You may feel weak and incapable of defending yourself. As a result, you may think you could be an easy target for abuse and manipulation.
- *Being easily triggered*: You could easily be triggered by minor misunderstandings and blow everything out of proportion and not according to what the other person intended. As a result, people will find it difficult to associate with you, even if they genuinely desire to be close to you. On your part, you may not even realize just how toxic you have actually become to other people. You may think that all you are doing is protecting yourself, whereas you are actually destroying any prospects

of people developing meaningful relationships with you.

- *Inability to communicate your feelings*: The basis of any meaningful relationship is communication. However, trauma survivors may find it hard to express their innermost feelings. If you were abused so that you couldn't speak out for some reason, you might grow up afraid to say no to the things you don't like. This often builds resentment toward even the closest people to you who mean you well. Negative feelings may build up inside you, and there are chances that these may explode at some point. When this happens, you may say or do things that will damage even your closest relationships.

As a result of the factors that we have just described, you may find it challenging to establish trust and intimacy with those who genuinely seek to be close to you. It would help if you communicated your fears, worries, and concerns so that others could know how to relate with you and get you the help you need. Trauma requires therapy so that you can reestablish meaningful relationships. Therapy helps you to understand that you are not in control of the past, but you can determine how the course of your actions will be from now on going forward.

THE PATH TO REBUILDING TRUST

For your relationships to develop, you need to build enough trust. It might take some time to incorporate people back into your life, especially after a traumatic experience. This is even more challenging if your trauma was caused by someone you trusted and they abused that assurance you had in them. In light of these concerns, the following guides can help you to rebuild trust in your new relationships:

- *Exercise patience with yourself*: Be sure to realize there is nothing wrong with feeling broken after your trust is breached. It takes some time for those negative feelings to wear away. However, realizing that the problem is with the abuser and not with you helps you to adjust much faster. Do not pressure yourself into committing to new relationships before you are ready. Allow yourself enough time to heal from your trauma until you feel ready to establish new relationships.
- *Establish healthy boundaries*: You should clearly express the boundaries of what you allow and what you do not tolerate. This could appear challenging if you have been traumatized by people who invalidate your needs or opinions over the years. However, this is an essential step that you cannot avoid if you are to establish meaningful relationships with people. Trust can

easily be built when people respect the healthy boundaries that you have established.

- *Exercise discretion*: The fact that you have opened yourself up to building new relationships doesn't mean you should allow everyone who wishes to be a part of your life. There are some people whom you will naturally get along with, while it will not be the same with others. Do not disregard your intuition if something doesn't feel right with someone. Having your trust breached when you seek to reestablish new relationships may shatter your hopes of ever letting people into your life again. Therefore, you need to remain careful. You have complete control over your life and can decide who to allow in and who to keep away. It is important to remember to protect your mental peace at all times by only allowing relationships with people who will help you rebuild trust in others.
- *Learn to forgive*: There are chances that the person who traumatized you sadly regrets their actions. Holding on to the wrongs they have done to you does not do you any good, nor does it allow you to move forward. First, forgive yourself and deliberately let go of resentment, feelings of revenge, or bitterness toward those who wronged you. This frees you mentally and allows you to heal quicker while opening vast possibilities for developing new relationships.

COMMUNICATION: A KEY TOOL IN HEALING RELATIONSHIPS

Trauma can make you feel unheard. You may also think that your opinions are not worthy of any consideration. If you have experienced traumatic abuse, your self-esteem might be negatively affected. This usually develops an unwillingness to communicate your feelings openly. Communicating your traumatic experiences to those around you helps them to understand your perspective better, making it easier for them to relate with you. Once you express clearly the things that traumatize you, people will most likely avoid bringing up the things that provoke or trigger you. This ensures that you heal effectively. Follow the tips given below so that your communication can improve to ensure better relationships:

- *Seek therapy first*: Before reconnecting to new relationships, you should first seek therapy to assess the current state of your psychological faculties. Trying to re-engage with people too soon may overwhelm you, depending on the nature and extent of your traumatic experiences. You may end up relapsing or overreacting to simple things, which delays your recovery. Once you can re-engage in healthy relationships with others, your therapist will let you know.
- *Positive body language* pushes people away from you. Be willing to show friendly and

accommodating body language to make others freely express themselves around you.

- *Be open and respectful*: Trauma can cause you to shut your feelings out as a defense mechanism to protect yourself from being attacked. This behavior is not helpful as it often causes resentment to build up as people offend you without knowing. Openly respectfully expressing yourself allows people to understand you better and act according to what makes you feel comfortable.
- *Pause before you talk and avoid speaking based on emotions*: Taking deep breaths can help calm yourself down before saying anything. Give yourself enough time to think carefully before you speak. It is essential to realize that most of your judgments have probably been compromised by your experiences. This may cause you to speak irrationally, especially if you are under the influence of your triggers.
- *Express your needs clearly*: Be self-aware to express yourself based on your preferences. Clarify all your boundaries without undermining those of others. Processing trauma sometimes leads to depression and confusion, leading you to say things contrary to what you mean. As such, be sure to be in the right frame of mind whenever you express your interests to be taken seriously.

- *Listen actively*: Allow others to speak without interrupting them so they will do the same when you talk. This helps to build clear understanding from a mutual perspective, making it easier for relationships to be established on even grounds.
- *Use "I" statements to clarify expressions instead of "you"*: "I" messages express personal feelings on specific issues and help avoid generalization. Good examples include "I feel" and "I want." If you use these types of statements, you can be sure that your dialogues will flow smoothly and clearly. Using "I" statements also helps to avoid defensiveness on the listener's part and prevent escalation of your dialogue that usually results from using confrontational "you" messages. For example, if you use the statement, "I don't appreciate this," instead of "You always do this," you can solicit better understanding and positive feedback.

SEEKING PROFESSIONAL HELP FOR RELATIONSHIP CHALLENGES

Therapy helps you shift from a state influenced by traumatic consequences to one in line with your sober mind. It involves working with a professional therapist to devise healthy strategies for coping with your fears and other associated emotions. Let's go through some of the features of professional therapy that contribute to its healing effects:

- *It provides a free space to open up on your issues*: Professional therapy gives you a free space to speak out about your traumatic experiences. Therapeutic dialogue is one of the most important steps toward your healing. Professional therapists are trained to direct you toward the best approach for handling your traumas at a pace you can manage. This leaves you in a better state to build and manage new relationships that you may form.
- *It enhances conflict management*: Professional therapy equips you with the ability to handle and resolve conflicts in ways beneficial to everyone involved. A therapist works closely with you and gets to understand your triggers, behavioral strengths, and weaknesses. Once they have such information about you, they will adjust your therapy sessions to equip you with personal strategies that help you resolve conflicts as you seek to build and maintain new relationships.
- *It helps to rebuild trust*: Trust is essential in forming your relationships' basis. If your traumatic experiences have been caused by the people you trusted, it may be difficult for you to believe in anyone again. Therapy helps you to realize that not everyone has bad intentions toward you,

which makes it easier to rebuild your trust with people.

Depending on the nature and extent of your trauma, you may decide to engage in group therapy sessions. This may help you to feel that you are not alone, as many other people are also going through trauma for different reasons. You might even find people to connect with who are more likely to understand you better. Two examples of group therapy types that you can benefit from are the following:

- *Couples therapy*: This is an intimate type of therapy that teaches you better ways of relating with your partner. The traumatic experiences that you went through are more likely to affect your romantic relationship in ways that are not obvious to you. When you go for couples therapy, be flexible because you may exhibit toxic behavior, not your partner. Couples therapy provides neutral mediation that allows you to see life clearly from your partner's perspective while also considering your own. This makes it easier for both of you to find a common ground which can be the basis of a lasting healthy relationship.
- *Family therapy*: You may need family therapy if your trauma affects the rest of your family members. Family therapy also applies when you are the only one being affected. Your family

members might not know how best to relate to you because of your condition. Therapy will enlighten your family members on how they can offer you the support you need. A therapist can help your family members develop better ways of relating with each other so that they unite as you recover from trauma.

CULTIVATING NEW RELATIONSHIPS POST-TRAUMA

After you emerge victorious from the trauma, you must establish new relationships to speed up your healing. The reason for therapy and treatment is for you to regain yourself so that you can integrate back into your family and society with less difficulty. This can initially be a challenge for you as you may need to learn how to incorporate people back into your life or be accepted into theirs. You can brace yourself for new relationships by applying some of the ideas that we are highlighting here:

- *Learn to socialize*: You can start by exposing yourself to activities involving many people you can selectively interact with. We recommend activities like volunteering or participating in social clubs, as these help you take responsibility for your behavior while also maintaining your personal freedom and discretion. Do not commit yourself to more interactions than you can bear.

Remember, connections will also require your time and input, which can be overwhelming if you engage in too many of them. Take each moment as it comes, and only expose yourself to situations that make you comfortable to maintain your mental stability.
- *Put more focus on developing yourself:* Focus more on developing your personal qualities so that you can give them out and have the same virtues reciprocated back to you in your relationships. Developing virtues like preserving self-respect, maintaining a calm mental state, and speaking positively about yourself improves your likelihood of exhibiting the same qualities to the people you connect and interact with.

Building healthy relationships after trauma is necessary for enhancing your recovery. You deserve new, fulfilling relationships with a network of supportive people around you. Healthy and effective ways of doing this include letting go of the trauma that you endured by forgiving your abusers and creating an open mind that is willing to explore new relationships. Practicing self-love by maintaining a calm mind and making positive affirmations about yourself also ensures you give the same virtues to those around you. This creates a basis for establishing healthy relationships. Professional therapy also helps you to develop some of the qualities that facilitate meaningful relationships. Remember to keep your mind and body healthy as you establish new relationships.

You can get more tips on how to do this by reading the next chapter, which focuses on self-care during trauma recovery.

8

NURTURING THE SELF—THE ART OF SELF-CARE IN TRAUMA RECOVERY

Shelly couldn't recall what happened after getting drunk and hitting a tree while sledding with her family and friends near a friend's house. Her kids were cared for by a friend while she visited the hospital and learned that she had lost her ability to taste and smell. She received physical and speech therapy at the rehabilitation hospital, improving her senses and ability to walk. Even though Shelly still had trouble with light and loudness, she recognized that something in herself had changed. She decided to be patient with herself, concentrate on one issue at a time, and refrain from comparing her accident to others. Shelly also benefits from support groups (AfterTrauma, n.d.-a).

This chapter emphasizes the importance of self-care in trauma recovery, urging readers to confront their emotions and avoid substance abuse. It provides tips for incorporating self-care into daily routines, promoting psychological, emotional, and physical wellness.

UNDERSTANDING SELF-CARE: MORE THAN JUST A BUZZWORD

Self-care refers to a person's, family's, or community's capacity to enhance their well-being, avoid sickness, maintain health, and manage illnesses and disabilities with or without the assistance of a health professional. To practice self-care, you should periodically check in with yourself and inquire about your physical, mental, and emotional health. Self-care routines will vary from person to person, and even how you define it may alter as time passes. Here are some essential aspects that you should understand about self-care:

- *Self-care is not a luxury*: Self-care goes beyond simple activities and involves making deliberate adjustments to your thoughts and actions that may harm your health. Examples include saying "no" without feeling guilty, understanding when to take a break, and avoiding unhealthy coping techniques. This essentially entails making informed choices that promote your well-being.
- *Self-care does not imply selfishness*: Self-care doesn't mean you should ignore other people's needs. It involves showing the same level of consideration and empathy for your needs as you do for those

you care about. Healthy limits and clear communication are vital components of self-care, which benefits you and makes you more accessible to those around you. You will feel more energized and able to do more for yourself and others when you set time for yourself, get adequate sleep, and work out.

- *Self-care is an ongoing process*: Self-care is a continuous practice involving caring for physical and mental demands, building resilience to deal with stress, and avoiding burnout. This makes it an essential part of daily life routines. Maintaining a healthy body and mind requires ongoing self-care, just as a garden needs regular watering to produce fresh fruits and vegetables.

The Art of Self-Care

A routine for self-care is when you decide to regularly reflect on your needs and make the necessary adjustments to fulfill them. Making self-care a priority begins with acknowledging your needs, including your mental state, physique, and friendships. You can start this process of reflection by engaging in easy exercises like writing, meditation, and mindfulness exercises. Making time for exercise each day, perhaps right before bed or a meal, is also great. Prioritizing self-care also includes

- recognizing that having needs is acceptable

- making room for mistakes
- taking care of your physical being by feeding it and incorporating exercise into your daily routine
- allowing yourself space to establish healthy boundaries
- expressing yourself lucidly and guilt-free
- keeping in touch with friends, places, and things that give you positive feelings

How to Formulate a Lasting Plan for Self-Care?

A self-care plan is a customized road map that aids stress management and lifestyle maintenance. It is a preventative technique that asks you to consider your needs and resources in times of difficulty. A plan also makes it easier for you to ask for assistance from individuals you feel comfortable with and makes you feel more in charge of your situation. Additionally, a self-care plan prevents solitude and fosters accountability and encouragement among your partners, thereby assisting you to stick to your schedules.

To create a plan:

1. Start modestly and build your routine over time to develop a sustainable self-care plan.
2. Try out various methods to see which one suits you the best.
3. List the things you think are good for you, and then do them.

Making a customized strategy requires awareness of your emotions and outcomes because only some plans work for everyone.

PHYSICAL SELF-CARE: NURTURING YOUR BODY

Some of the most fundamental requirements for good health are met by taking care of your body. You may have various negative effects if you start skipping meals, not sleeping well, or developing harmful habits like smoking. In the future, you might also develop long-term chronic diseases due to your lifestyle, or you might even start to feel crankier and more worn out. Unattended stress may result in caregiver burnout, described as chronic physical and emotional tiredness from providing care.

Daily physical wellness maintenance has both short- and long-term advantages. You'll avoid many health problems, have a strong foundation for self-care, and be in good enough physical condition to look after the people you care about. Let's look at some tips for maintaining your physical health.

Make a Healthy Diet a Priority

"You are what you eat," as the saying goes. The meals you eat provide the energy your body requires for optimal performance. If you mainly eat junk food and takeout, the odds are that you'll feel weak and fatigued throughout the day. This is partly why you must eat nutritious meals in your daily life. These include fresh whole foods rich in nutrients that will give your body the energy it requires for peak performance. Healthy comfort food options provide sustenance and a warm atmosphere. Vegetable soups, mashed cauliflower, whole-grain spaghetti, roasted sweet potatoes, and chicken tenders cooked in the oven are a few examples. For a fulfilling experience, pick healthy products, apply cooking techniques, and manage portion sizes.

Exercise Frequently

Living a sedentary lifestyle increases the risk of diseases like colon cancer, high blood pressure, heart disease, diabetes, and osteoporosis. Regular exercise promotes mental health by producing endorphins, lowering anxiety, and enhancing cognitive function. Exercise helps your body deal with stress by controlling the fight-or-flight response, increasing the immune system, and improving digestion.

Sleep Enough

In today's fast-paced environment, getting seven to nine hours of sleep per night is critical for general wellness (Families for Depression Awareness, 2021). Set a healthy nightly routine that includes putting away mobile devices, playing soothing sounds, sipping calming green tea, participating in relaxing hobbies, and practicing deep breathing. This will assist your mind and body relax, improving the quality and quantity of your sleep.

Outdoor Strolls

Connecting with nature is another effective method for enhancing your sense of well-being. Spending more time outside lowers stress levels improves emotions, sharpens mental agility, and lowers the chance of developing depression and anxiety. Additionally, walking outdoors exposes you to more natural light, boosting your vitamin D levels.

Doctor Visits and Taking Medication

Maintaining excellent health and avoiding serious health difficulties requires regular doctor visits and mental health treatment. If you are on a prescription, use a pill holder to store your pills and set a daily alarm to remind you when to take them. Apps like MyTherapy are also available to download, as they help you schedule different times to take your medications.

Drink Water

All biological functions, including the excretion of toxins, depend on water. It might surprise you that many people neglect to consume adequate water. To remind yourself to sip water frequently, have a one-liter bottle nearby. Additionally, pay attention to your body's indicators and sip water anytime you feel dehydrated.

Water has been proven to naturally have relaxing properties because of treating the negative effects of dehydration on the body and brain. A crucial component of anxiety management is getting enough water to drink. Having adequate water can make you feel relaxed, even if you are not anxious (Solara Mental Health, n.d.).

EMOTIONAL SELF-CARE: TENDING TO YOUR EMOTIONAL GARDEN

Cristiana and her partner relocated to England in 2015 in search of a better life together and with plans to get engaged. However, on February 16th, she was injured in an accident that left her in a coma and admitted to the Royal London Hospital's trauma department. Cristiana was run over by a truck and underwent a protracted and challenging rehabilitation process because of severe pelvis and leg injuries that required tracheostomy tube placement. The physiotherapist, Tom, was Cristiana's hero for helping her sit, stand, and walk. Cristiana underwent more surgery after returning to Romania, which is why she is still unable to walk. Nine months later, Cristiana's boyfriend broke up with her. She remained resilient, and though it was hard, she understood that the most crucial thing was to survive and recover with the help of her family, friends, physicians, and nurses around her (After-Trauma, n.d.-b).

Emotional self-care is recognizing and acknowledging feelings, thoughts, and behaviors and finding healthy outlets for them. It entails dealing with stress, expressing emotions, and cultivating positive emotions. Many people suppress negative feelings, resulting in unfulfilled lives and an inability to comprehend why. The more you subdue your feelings, the more difficult healing from trauma becomes.

The ability to face problems and cultivate self-assurance positively affects emotional well-being. Negative emotions can negatively impact your body, mind, and social life by causing feelings of overload, irritability, and difficulties coping with day-to-day challenges, in addition to the trauma you are already experiencing.

According to studies, chronic emotional conflict can worsen inflammation, which has been related to diseases like cancer, metabolic problems, and cardiovascular diseases (The Human Condition, 2022). Individuals suffering from cancer benefit from emotional self-care because it helps them embrace change, uphold their everyday lives, and maintain their identity. Here are some of the advantages that emotional self-care can provide:

- *Greater adaptability and balance*: Those who take care of their emotional health can withstand hardship and manage life's inevitable challenges. Emotional self-care can also assist people in finding a balance between their internal and outside lives. Taking a holistic approach to your health promotes mental and physical equilibrium.
- *Enhanced interactions*: The emotional support of a partner is often necessary for many people. The

fact that overdependence on a partner can strain relationships cannot be overstated, as with Christiana. Being aware of your emotions also helps you communicate more effectively, which will build deeper and more genuine relationships. Meaningful relationships can positively contribute to your healing process.

Emotional Self-Care Methods

Emotional self-care involves being attentive, practicing acceptance, setting boundaries, using constructive self-talk, and getting sufficient rest. All this can be achieved through the following emotional self-care techniques:

- *Record it in a journal*: Sometimes, you're just not prepared to discuss what you are going through. However, holding your feelings in is not a good idea. Journaling and expressing your emotions on paper is a fantastic option.
- *Work on your acceptance and mindfulness*: A variety of emotions are felt by people when they are going through post-traumatic stress. Recognizing and acknowledging your genuine emotions rather than suppressing or rejecting them is essential. Always remember that self-criticism is counterproductive. The ability to accept all your feelings and be present in the moment is made possible by practicing self-acceptance. Find

healthy ways to express your emotions, whether good or bad.
- *Create and uphold healthy boundaries:* Emotional self-care involves learning how to say no" to commitments that aren't in your best interests or that can disrupt necessary "me time." Taking time to consider the existing boundaries and those that need to be established can be beneficial. When the occasion calls for it, you should communicate these boundaries. Once boundaries have been established, it's vital to continually uphold them despite any inconvenience or discomfort.
- *Self-care through therapy:* Therapy can assist in determining the underlying causes of self-care failures, such as codependency, depression, and dementia. It can increase mood, ease symptoms, and impart new communication and coping mechanisms. You can develop ways to deal with dementia by continuing to practice self-care.
- *Use uplifting self-talk*: Although we have no influence over what other people say about us or to us, we do have power over how we talk and listen to ourselves. Emotional self-care includes developing healthy and supportive communication with yourself, just as you would with someone you deeply care about.
- *Permit rest*: Everybody needs a few moments to relax and take a break; operating continuously at a high rate of speed all day is unhealthy. When

necessary, pause for a moment. Taking a nap or engaging in some sort of relaxation could give you the break you need.

Use Your Five Senses for Emotional Self-Care

- *Sound*: Excellent grounding tactics include playing your favorite song loudly, making a call to a close friend, or even reading a book aloud.
- *Touch*: Grounding yourself through touch may involve having a warm bath, hugging a furry friend, or bursting bubble wrap.
- *Smell*: Lighting aromatic candles, inhaling peppermint, or applying scented oils with uplifting connotations can all be soothing grounding techniques.
- *Taste*: You can ground yourself by chewing on a mint, biting into an orange, or eating chocolate.
- *Sight*: Grounding techniques include concentrating on items, such as counting the objects around you, streaming your favorite movie, or reading.

Support Groups and Relationships

According to the Mayo Clinic, social support is essential for mental health and resiliency (Mayo Clinic, 2020). Joining support groups, contacting loved ones, or interacting with individuals on online platforms such as 7 Cups can all be beneficial. The following is a thorough example of how to incorporate help into your self-care:

- *Develop good connections*: Maintain wholesome connections by surrounding yourself with upbeat, encouraging people. Develop deep bonds with your family and friends.
- *Seek social support*: When you require assistance or a listening ear, speak with close friends or loved ones you can trust. Sharing your thoughts and feelings can help you feel better.
- *Forming or joining a group of supporters*: In a support group, you can privately share your feelings and experiences with others who understand you, offer constructive criticism, and won't pass judgment.
- *Social media*: Many online platforms have evolved into support groups that will let you interact, exchange experiences, and offer one another emotional support, improving mental health and well-being.

BALANCING SELF-CARE WITH LIFE'S DEMANDS

Understanding your responsibilities in life is crucial to strike a balance between self-care and other commitments. The four basic kinds of commitments in life are your loved ones, school, job, and social activities.

- *Family*: Family responsibilities can include looking after young or elderly relatives, reunions with relatives, and keeping in touch with friends and extended families. Balancing family responsibilities and self-care can be challenging, but it is crucial to prevent burnout and tiredness.
- *School*: Commitments related to school involve attending lectures, finishing projects, and preparing for tests. It might be challenging to juggle the responsibilities of being a university student with self-care, but it is necessary if you want to succeed academically.
- *Work*: Completing tasks, attending meetings, and sticking to due dates are all part of the job. Maintaining a healthy work–life balance is essential to preventing burnout and maintaining performance. Setting limits, taking breaks, and prioritizing self-care routines outside of your job can all help with this.
- *Social activities*: Participating in social gatherings or spending time with your peers are examples of social commitments. The benefits of social

connection for mental wellness should not be underestimated, but self-care should always come first. Setting restrictions, putting downtime first, and carefully choosing your social contacts are vital.

How to Balance Life's Obligations and Self-Care

A life imbalance can negatively impact mental well-being, cortisol levels, sleep quality, life satisfaction, relationships, and irritability. Consider making efforts to relieve stress through meal kits, regular exercise, and virtual therapy for anxiety, sadness, and burnout. Having coffee, watching movies, or taking a break are all simple ways to find time for yourself. Despite how busy and stressful life can be, finding a balance can help with long-term emotions and general well-being.

Setting limits, assigning responsibilities to others, planning, and prioritizing activities are all applicable strategies. Delegating responsibilities frees up time for self-care activities, and asking for help from loved ones, friends, or professionals can bring emotional support and self-care strategy advice. By employing these techniques, you can maintain a healthy balance and good mental health.

Know When to Get Professional Help

Although self-care might assist you in lessening and overcoming trauma, it cannot replace professional assistance. Seek treatment if you think a traumatic event is affecting your life. The same applies when the trauma seems to stick around for too long. Various treatment options are available, including CBT, which assists in recognizing and replacing unhealthy emotions with better ones.

This chapter focused more on nurturing the self, which promotes self-care for trauma recovery by focusing on your well-being, illness prevention, and management through informed choices. In addition to self-care, this also includes forming boundaries, creating clear communication, and using personalized stress management strategies.

9

THE SILVER LINING—EMBRACING POST-TRAUMATIC GROWTH

Kay Wilson's harrowing journey began when she and her friend were attacked by terrorists while working as tour guides in Jerusalem. Kay, aged 46, survived a traumatic incident in 2010 where she saw the death of a friend and endured brutal stab wounds. To find solace and strength, she played the song "Somewhere Over the Rainbow" by Judy Garland in her mind. Despite severe physical and psychological trauma, Kay has since emerged with a renewed appreciation for life and a determination to combat hatred.

Having recovered from her physical wounds, Kay now shares her survival story with varying audiences worldwide to dispel hatred and promote understanding. She finds purpose in making meaning out of the senselessness of her ordeal and is currently working on a book based on what she experienced. Although Kay grapples with flashbacks and survivor's guilt, her journey embodies PTG as she discovers her strength and a profound focus on assisting others.

Through her resilience and determination, Kay Wilson inspires others to find positive change in the aftermath of trauma. Her story serves as a testament to the human spirit's capacity for healing, resilience, and the pursuit of a greater purpose (Collier, 2016).

This chapter will explore the concept of PTG and how it can lead to powerful personal transformation. It will also delve into the idea that traumatic experiences have the potential to catalyze profound changes in individuals, ultimately leading them to cultivate a life of deeper meaning and purpose.

UNRAVELING POST-TRAUMATIC GROWTH

PTG is an ideology that emerged in the mid-1990s and is the brainchild of Richard Tedeschi and Lawrence Calhoun (Collier, 2016). PTG explains the transformative process that can occur following trauma, where individuals who undergo psychological struggle in the aftermath of adversity often experience positive personal growth. PTG involves the development of new self-perceptions, enhanced understanding of the world, improved interpersonal relationships, a reimagined future, and a deeper appreciation of life (Tedeschi & Calhoun, 1996). It highlights how you can emerge from trauma with a newfound resilience and a broader perspective on your life and the world around you.

When you face trauma, PTG can shake your core beliefs and challenge your understanding of the world around you. However, through that process, you can develop new insights, perspectives, and ways of relating to yourself and others. It is not about erasing the pain or forgetting the past but integrating the trauma into your life story and finding meaning and purpose in the face of adversity.

Compassion is related to PTG. Having experienced suffering, you may develop a heightened empathy and understanding for the struggles of others. Additionally, resilience is a key outcome of PTG. It involves adapting to and bouncing back from adversity while developing the ability to cope with future challenges. PTG helps you to build psychological and emotional resources that enable you to navigate life's difficulties with greater strength and resilience.

Post-Traumatic Growth Versus Resilience

Resilience and PTG are two distinct processes that arise from facing difficult experiences. Resilience involves being flexible and optimistic and utilizing available resources, such as coping strategies and social support, to overcome adversity (Yao & Hsieh, 2019). On the other hand, PTG goes beyond mere resilience. It occurs when individuals use their challenging experiences as opportunities for personal growth and development. Rather than simply returning to their pre-traumatic state, they find meaning in their struggles and emerge as better versions of themselves.

PTG encompasses various aspects of personal transformation. It involves understanding life deeply, forming stronger relationships, making spiritual or existential changes, discovering a heightened sense of strength, and realizing new possibilities (Joseph, 2009). For instance, someone who has experienced the loss of a loved one may re-evaluate the importance of relationships and foster stronger bonds with family and friends, thereby increasing their social support network (Calhoun & Tedeschi, 2014). This process allows individuals to learn from their adversities and reshape their perceptions of themselves, their lives, and the world around them.

A study involving 420 college students found that perceived PTG was associated with improved emotion recognition, while resilience negatively correlated with empathy in 2010. However, PTG did not correlate with empathy. The results suggest that PTG may be linked to cognitive ability and personal growth in relationships. The study emphasizes the impact of contextual factors on empathy and emotion recognition, suggesting the need for further research in this area (Elam & Taku, 2022). While interconnected, they represent different ways of responding to and navigating traumatic experiences. Both processes significantly understand how individuals respond to and thrive in facing challenges.

THE FIVE DOMAINS OF POST-TRAUMATIC GROWTH

Research suggests that approximately 70% of individuals encounter at least one potentially traumatic event during their lifetime (Benjet et al., 2016). According to Tedeschi and Calhoun (1996), when measuring PTG, they often look at five main areas. These include improvements in your relationships, a stronger sense of personal strength, the discovery of new possibilities in life, the evolution of your spirituality, and a deeper appreciation of life. Seeing how you can experience growth and positive changes even after difficult and traumatic events is fascinating. Let's look at the five domains in greater depth:

- *Greater appreciation of life*: Following a traumatic event, you may undergo a transformative shift in your perspective, leading to a profound appreciation for life. This newfound awareness and gratitude can arise from a realization of the fragility of life and recognizing the resilience and strength needed to overcome adversity. As a result, you may find yourself savoring the simple joys, cherishing meaningful connections, and being more present in the immediate moment. This greater appreciation of life can serve as a foundation for personal growth, fostering a sense of purpose and a desire to live life to the fullest.

- *Closer relationships*: Trauma can sometimes lead to stronger and more meaningful connections with others. You may seek support from loved ones and experience deeper understanding and empathy within your relationships.
- *Increased personal strength*: Facing and overcoming adversity can reveal inner reservoirs of strength and resilience. You may discover newfound capabilities and a sense of personal empowerment you did not realize you possessed.
- *Recognition of new possibilities*: Traumatic experiences can shift your perspective and open up new opportunities or previously unexplored paths. You may develop a fresh outlook on life, find alternative solutions, and embrace possibilities you hadn't considered before.
- *Spiritual development*: Some individuals experience spiritual growth following trauma. This could involve deepening their spiritual beliefs or searching for meaning and purpose in life. They may find solace, guidance, or a connection with something greater than themselves.

You should note that these domains of PTG are not experienced by everyone in the same way or to the same extent. The journey of growth and recovery is unique to each individual and can vary based on their circumstances and resilience.

Traumatic Experiences Give Birth to Personal Strength

Trauma survivors often uncover hidden abilities and strengths they were unaware of before the unfortunate incidents they encountered. Consider the inspiring story of Malala Yousafzai, a Pakistani education advocate who made history in 2014 as the youngest Nobel Peace Prize laureate. Her remarkable journey began when she bravely survived an assassination attempt orchestrated by the Taliban. Even from a young age, Malala passionately championed girls' education, which drew the attention of the Taliban, who posed a grave threat to her life.

On October 9, 2012, a gunman targeted her while returning home from school as a student. Astonishingly, Malala survived the attack and persevered in her mission to promote education. In 2013, she delivered a poignant speech at the United Nations and authored her debut book, *I Am Malala* (Kale, 2021).

Malala Yousafzai's inspiring story teaches us that trauma survivors can discover remarkable abilities and strengths within themselves. Malala's resilience and determination to promote education, even in grave danger, is truly inspiring. Her experience shows us that adversity can uncover a deep well of courage, passion, and purpose. It teaches us that there is potential for growth and positive change even in the darkest times. Malala's story reminds us of the power of resilience, the importance of standing up for what we believe in, and the transformative impact trauma can have on shaping our lives and the lives of others.

FOSTERING TRAUMATIC GROWTH: STRATEGIES FOR TRANSFORMATION

Journaling is a fantastic tool for fostering PTG. It is like having a personal therapist right at your fingertips. It is helpful for the following:

- *Processing emotions*: Writing in a journal lets you let it all out. You can pour your heart onto the pages and process those intense emotions of going through a traumatic experience. It is a safe space to be raw and honest about your feelings.
- *Reflecting on experiences*: Journaling provides an opportunity for deep reflection on your experiences. If you put your thoughts and emotions into words, you can revisit past events, explore how they have influenced you, and gain fresh insights. Journaling offers a space for introspection and self-discovery, allowing you to process your thoughts and emotions in a meaningful way. Through journaling, you can uncover hidden meanings, identify patterns, and gain a deeper understanding of yourself and your experiences.

- *Tracking progress*: One of the coolest things about journaling is that it lets you track your progress over time. You can reflect on your previous entries and see how far you've come.

Expressive writing is a potent tool for healing and transformation (Payne, 2023). Dr. Marich emphasizes the therapeutic advantages of capturing thoughts and emotions through writing. Through expressive writing, individuals can experience substantial strides in their healing journeys.

Post-Traumatic Growth Through Mindfulness and Meditation

Mindfulness and meditation act as superpowers when facilitating PTG. They offer incredible tools for healing and self-discovery. Picture mindfulness as your compass that helps you stay present and engaged with your experiences after trauma. It's all about consciously focusing on the *here-and-now* moment without judgment. When you practice mindfulness, you create a safe space to explore your thoughts, emotions, and bodily sensations connected to your trauma. Mindfulness lets you fully embrace your thoughts and feelings without getting overwhelmed.

Meditation is a wonderful practice for cultivating mindfulness. Through meditation, you can tap into a sense of inner calmness and resilience that can be incredibly empowering. What is remarkable is that there are now apps available, like Insight Timer and MyLife Meditation, that offer a variety of guided meditations specifically tailored for trauma survivors. These guided meditations can be valuable, providing support and guidance as you continue your healing journey. They offer a range of options to choose from so you can find meditations that resonate with you and address your specific needs.

The Role of Building Supportive Relationships in Post-Traumatic Growth

Attaining the support of your loved ones, such as family and friends, is crucial. Their presence and understanding can provide you with the strength and bravery needed to confront the challenges that come with recovering from trauma. Your friends and family can lend a listening ear, provide comfort, and remain steadfast by your side as you progress through the highs and lows of your healing journey. Their unwavering support becomes an anchor that keeps you grounded and helps you find your way through the healing process. In other words, they're your ultimate cheerleaders, always there to lift you and remind you that you are not alone.

In addition, being part of support groups can make a significant difference. These groups offer a sense of community and a shared understanding that can be incredibly valuable. It is reminiscent of finding people who have walked a similar path and truly *get* what you're experiencing. Support groups, like the ones provided by the Sidran Institute, create a safe space where you can freely express yourself, share your story, and learn from others who have been through similar situations. It is a place where you can feel genuinely heard, validated, and supported. You get to connect with individuals who understand your unique challenges and offer a network of empathy, guidance, and encouragement. Being part of a support group can give you a sense of belonging and remind you that you're not alone in your journey toward healing and growth.

EMBRACING YOURSELF: THE TRANSFORMATIONAL POWER OF TRAUMA

A traumatic experience can push you to grow in ways you never thought possible. It can ignite a journey of self-discovery, resilience, and strength. When you go through the healing process, you learn to adapt, cope, and find new ways of living and thriving. You may discover hidden reservoirs of inner strength that you didn't know existed within you.

Trauma can also deepen the extent to which you understand yourself and others. It can cultivate empathy and compassion within you as you recognize the pain and struggles faced by others who have gone through similar experiences. This newfound understanding can lead to a greater ability to develop meaningful connections and a desire to make a positive impact in the lives of others.

It is good to approach PTG with patience and self-compassion. If you embrace the opportunity for growth, you can emerge from the shadows of trauma as a stronger, wiser, and more compassionate individual. You can reclaim your life and create a new narrative reflecting your resilience and the lessons you have learned. Remember, your trauma does not define you. You have the power to shape your own story and rewrite the narrative of your life. With determination, support, and self-belief, you can move forward and harness the transformative potential that lies within you.

Ric Elias was a US Airways Flight 1549 passenger the "Miracle on the Hudson," in 2009. The plane suffered engine failure after hitting geese, but Captain Sully successfully landed it on the Hudson River, saving everyone on board. This experience had a profound impact on Elias, prompting him to reflect on life's priorities and the fragility of life.

It was a life-altering experience that taught him three valuable lessons. He learned that life can change in an instant. He realized the importance of not postponing what truly matters and embraced a sense of urgency and purpose. He also regretted wasting time in 2009. Elias eliminated negativity and prioritized positive relationships. He shifted from being right to choosing happiness and fostering healthier connections.

Another thing he learned is to value fatherhood deeply. He recognized the significance of being a great dad. This realization reshaped his priorities and led him to cherish those precious moments. Through his transformative journey, Ric Elias inspires us to reflect on our own lives, prioritize what truly matters, and live with intention and gratitude (Elias, 2023).

Embracing Grief and Transformation After a Traumatic Experience

It is entirely normal to feel a sense of grief after going through a traumatic experience. When something big happens in your life that turns everything upside down, it's natural to long for the person you used to be before it all happened. It's okay to miss your old self and mourn the life you had before everything changed. Your feelings of loss and sadness are valid. During the healing process, you will need to be gentle with yourself. There is no right or wrong timeline for moving forward. It's advisable to take the necessary time and space to process our emotions, reflect on the past, and slowly adapt to the changes brought about by the trauma.

Allowing yourself to grieve and acknowledging the pain can be essential to the healing process. This way, you can honor your past self, the experiences you've lost, and the person you once were. If you embrace this grief, you create space for acceptance and growth.

You need to remember that healing is not linear. Some days may be more challenging than others, and that is fine. You may fluctuate between moments of strength and vulnerability, but cultivate patience. Sharing your experiences and emotions with those who understand you can provide validation and comfort.

Embrace the Journey of Post-Traumatic Growth

PTG is not something that happens instantly. It is a process that unfolds over time, like a journey you embark on. It is about embracing the path of transformation and personal development rather than solely focusing on the result. During this journey, you should recognize and celebrate every small step of progress you make. Each tiny bit of growth and healing is a testament to your strength and resilience. Sometimes, it might feel like you're not progressing as much as you'd prefer. There will be ups and downs along the way, which is perfectly okay.

Embracing PTG means being open to change and finding meaning in the process. It is about learning from your experiences and allowing them to shape your perspectives positively. It's also an opportunity to discover inner strengths and capabilities that you may not have realized you possessed. There is no right or wrong way to go about it. It is about finding what works best for you and being open to exploring different avenues of healing and self-discovery.

As you continue this journey, being kind and compassionate to yourself is important. Acknowledge and celebrate the small wins and derive motivation and self-confidence from them. Let us go to the next chapter, "A Brighter Tomorrow," where we will discuss strategies to maintain progress in your trauma recovery, handle setbacks, and embrace a future with resilience and empowerment.

10

A BRIGHTER TOMORROW— STAYING ON THE PATH OF HEALING

Recovery from trauma is a journey that begins in your mind. The memories of the traumatic experiences that you may have gone through only reside in your mind. This is the first place to start caring for yourself to recover and reignite your vision for a brighter tomorrow. Although this may be hard, you will more likely enjoy the results if you can start working on your mind today.

The story of Lisa is inspiring and shows the power of being hopeful in the face of trauma in a bid to ensure a brighter tomorrow. On her way home, Lisa could not lift her arm. She was rushed into the Emergency Room, where she was told she had an infection in her arm from using and had to go into surgery immediately or she would lose her arm. She underwent both orthopedic and trauma surgery to help her recover. To revive her hopes of living a normal life again, Lisa's doctors asked her about who she wished to become after recovering so that they could keep her mind fixed on the prospects of getting better. Lisa had two kids and kept reaffirming that she would return to her kids again and didn't want to leave them without a mother. She also expressed her desire to run to keep her body fit physically. The doctors were glad that she was optimistic, but they didn't quite know whether her wishes would be possible because of the extent of her injuries.

Against all odds, Lisa gradually managed to recover from the trauma, and the doctors were able to save her arm. She returned home to her children. You, too, can recover from trauma and ignite your hopes for a brighter tomorrow if you affirm it and keep a positive mind. Get more information on how you can get this done by reading this chapter.

STAYING THE COURSE: MAINTAINING PROGRESS IN HEALING

While you are recovering, it is essential for you to realize that your body and mind are not yet in their best state. There will undoubtedly be limitations in how you do certain things, even as you constantly try to improve. This is because trauma affects many parts of your mind and body, and restoring them to normal might take some time to materialize. The whole process will require a lot of patience. Do not pressure yourself to quickly overcome all your traumas because that might slow your recovery.

You can use several strategies to help you cope better with the pressure of desiring to see quick results. One such strategy that has been proven useful is the Seinfeld Strategy. This strategy is named after Jerry Seinfeld, a comedian who is credited for its application.

In 1998, Jerry Seinfeld was reported by Forbes magazine to have earned an estimated $267 million (Clear, 2013). He attributed his success to several principles, which later became part of what is known as the Seinfeld Strategy. The Seinfeld Strategy focuses on avoiding procrastination and consistency once you start working toward something. To practice it, list clear plans on a task you want to fulfill before getting a wall calendar. Find a colored marker and label each day on the calendar that you work toward your goal with an "X." The idea behind the Seinfeld Strategy is to keep the chain of Xs growing without breaking it so that it inspires you to maintain consistency.

The Seinfeld Strategy deliberately leaves out any accountability on the results, whether you manage to carry out your task to perfection or otherwise, just as long as you work toward it each day. On your journey to recovery, you can put in place realistic goals and targets alongside reasonable time frames for completing them. After that, apply the Seinfeld Strategy to keep you on course. Your mind is naturally inclined toward subconsciously adopting consistent patterns as a normal way of thinking. Suppose you intentionally cultivate positive thinking habits aligned with the future you want to live in while you are still recovering. In that case, you will undoubtedly be an achiever, even post-trauma.

In addition to applying the Seinfeld Strategy, self-reflection helps you align with the plans you have put in place. Self-reflection helps you to achieve the following:

- *Identify patterns*: Self-reflection helps you identify patterns that align with your behavior so that you can be accountable for them. Healing from trauma requires you to realize that the negative experiences that you went through are not a part of you, so you shouldn't act in line with them. If you identify any behavioral patterns that align with the trauma that you experienced, the awareness that comes with self-reflection helps you to make relevant changes.
- *Track your progress*: Continuously identifying your behavior patterns helps evaluate your progress. With more personal accountability, you can determine whether you are moving forward, not progressing, or actually going backward. Regardless of the state of your progress, it's important to remember that your recovery is a process with both positive and negative

experiences, which only need to be accounted for so that you can make the necessary amendments.

- *Make the required adjustments*: Once you track your progress, you can make the desired changes according to your recovery. This step does not require your therapist since only you know what feels best for you. Holding yourself accountable for your progress shows that you are recovering well. This will help you make the necessary adjustments to ensure a better response to your traumas.
- *Journal your activities*: When you self-reflect, you can engage in journaling, which is a practice that helps you to express your innermost feelings and thoughts. It involves noting down all these details in a book or on paper. Journaling improves the clarity of your recovery journey and the future that is more likely to be created by your habits. Journaling may help you determine the reasons behind your actions and why you need to shift your focus when needed.

Your healing process and journey toward a brighter future is unique for you. You might wonder how you will navigate through some of the triggers when you face them after your recovery. It is expected to be triggered even after successful therapy. People respond differently to therapy, considering that your recovery will depend on several other factors concerning your individuality. It will be quite helpful if you identify your potential triggers, especially after journaling, and discover new ways of dealing with them.

You can also talk to the people whom you are comfortable with, including your therapist and loved ones, so that they can help you devise practical ways of minimizing your exposure to the things that trigger you. Properly managing your setbacks is essential to your overall healing.

TURNING SETBACKS INTO COMEBACKS

As you are healing, it helps to identify yourself as a survivor, not a victim of trauma, without blaming yourself. This helps you not to dwell much on the thoughts that you could have done better to prevent your traumatic experiences from happening in the first place. Self-blame is not good because it increases the likelihood of flashbacks on your way to living a new life.

One of the challenges you could also face is the prospect of reintegrating normally into your family and society. You might have to meet the people or situations that trigger traumatic memories. It is essential that you understand that this is normal, but you will need to be resilient. You will be better positioned to deal with post-trauma setbacks if you acknowledge that they are a normal part of the healing process.

The life story of the successful business tycoon Richard Branson is a source of inspiration to use your setbacks as an opportunity to develop better strategies for overcoming your challenges. Branson had dyslexia as a young boy, a scenario that caused a reduced ability to read, write, and properly grasp academic concepts. He dropped out of high school at 16 and had a very poor school resume at that time. However, Branson was excellent at connecting and relating with people, which became the basis of his first Uber business. He established a student newspaper endorsed by rock stars, politicians, and other celebrities, symbolizing his rise to stardom and riches. Branson once said, "You need to learn from your failures and take them as an opportunity to start all over again without being embarrassed by them."

Here are some of the strategies that you can use to handle the setbacks that you may encounter during your recovery:

- *Reach out to a supportive network*: With a group of people supporting you on your journey to recovery, it becomes easier to handle the setbacks you may encounter, especially those related to relapsing. A peer group of colleagues recovering from trauma gives you a realistic basis to rest your expectations. If others are going through similar experiences as you, yet they manage to continue along their journey to recovery, so can you. Please

note that this does not undermine your individuality and that your progress in healing can be different from that of others. However, you can still derive encouragement from those who are making it.
- *Reconsider some successful strategies that have worked for you*: You will indeed have other things you have managed to heal from in the past. When you face setbacks or relapses, consider the strategies that previously worked for you and try reapplying them.
- *Practice self-compassion*: Self-compassion involves exercising patience and constantly encouraging yourself to improve. Also, you may refer to times when you overcame some setbacks, even before the traumatic experience. Be kind to yourself and avoid blaming yourself for what you went through.
- *Utilize tools that help to manage anxiety and stress*: Activities like aromatherapy, nature walks, meditation, and other body and mind relaxation techniques can relieve you of stress and anxiety, leaving you feeling better.
- *Celebrate the small milestones you achieve along the way*: Whenever you successfully overcome a trigger or avoid relapsing into something that you previously found challenging to beat, reward yourself for the success. This motivates your mind to feel good about the process and to keep the

momentum. The Journey app is a helpful tool that you can use to keep a record of your successes along the way.

THE ROAD AHEAD: EMBRACING AN EMPOWERED FUTURE

As you recover from trauma, your present challenges are only temporary. Once you recover, you will soon get rid of them to live your desired life. Your traumatic experiences do not determine what you should or shouldn't do. Instead, you can accomplish the life you want if you allow your vision for the future to determine the course of action you take today as you are still healing.

As you visualize your goals for the future, be sure to write them down. Also, create a course of action as you work toward your goals. This helps to keep you focused when you face temporary setbacks like triggers or relapsing episodes. You can use vision boards to note your goals and course of action. A vision board visually represents your goals and the steps you intend to take to achieve them. You can use a digital vision board or a manual to write your plans. Create a vision board when your mind is clear so that you don't set goals based on temporary emotions that don't represent what you want.

PTG refers to positive psychological transformation after trauma. Various ways determine how much you have undergone PTG, as the American Psychological Association outlines. Self-report scales are personal scorecards that you can use to evaluate your growth in personal relationships, spirituality, gratitude for life, and the prospects of bringing your dreams to reality (Collier, 2016). Developing these attributes will help you to bring meaning to your new life after trauma. Here are some of their descriptions:

- *Development of personal strength*: This attribute is evaluated based on your feedback as the trauma survivor. Your ability to reframe negative experiences into positive ones is a sign of personal strength. The same applies to the development of emotional resilience.
- *Ability to foster and maintain new relationships*: Relating better with people around you after trauma is a sign that can be used to weigh your PTG.
- *Wider possibilities for life*: Your ability to envision yourself achieving better things for your life beyond your current challenging experiences is a positive sign of PTG. When you can anticipate unlimited possible outcomes for your dreams, you are on the right track to a brighter future.
- *Spiritual growth*: Embracing your spiritual beliefs is a sign that you have hope for the future beyond your traumatic experiences.
- *Gratitude for life*: A general appreciation of what you experience is a positive sign of PTG. To

practice daily gratitude, we recommend using the Five Minute Journal app.

Gabby Giffords, a former Arizona congresswoman, survived an assassination attempt after being shot in the head in 2011 (Simons, 2022). She was shot in the brain areas that control speech and coordination. Her case is an excellent example of PTG, as Gabby regained a positive outlook on life during her recovery by resuming the things she loves doing. These include advocating for gun control, meeting people, and occasionally singing, which are all positive signs of PTG.

YOUR LIFELONG COMPANION: CULTIVATING RESILIENCE

Resilience describes your ability to withstand the mental impact of the things that provoke a negative emotional response in line with the traumatic experiences that you went through (Nugent et al., 2014). Resilience is an ability that you develop over time. It is a skill that you consciously master as you adapt to stressful situations. You cannot be treated or counseled to develop resilience; you must develop it through sheer mental toughness.

According to Kanako Taku from Oakland University, resilience differs from PTG (Collier, 2016). Resilience keeps developing as a function of time beyond PTG. The following can help you build and maintain your resilience to traumatic memories:

- *Practice good self-care*: To build and maintain resilience, you must focus only on what benefits your emotional, physical, and psychological well-being. Keep your mind away from the disturbing memories by feeding it with pleasant thoughts. Doing this gradually develops a natural barrier against traumatic thoughts over time.
- *Keep a strong support network*: Maintain close association with like-minded people who may also be working toward developing their resilience. Having such people around you is likely to push you to keep improving. Linking up with others on platforms like Eventbrite and Meetup also helps to widen your network. On such platforms, you are more likely to meet people working toward developing their resilience, which helps keep you focused.
- *Challenge your limits*: Stretch yourself to keep improving by accepting to deal with your traumatic experiences directly. This is, however, not a substitute for professional help, which you certainly need to seek if your trauma is severe. To challenge your limits, you can train your mind by exposing it to what previously triggered you until you become numb to those provocations. This takes time and can be likened to the growth of the

bamboo tree, which first develops its roots over several years before sprouting. You can also keep developing your resilience until you are ready to reconnect with the world.

Sharing with others about your work toward mental resilience will also empower them to develop their own as they learn from you. Platforms like Medium and Facebook can host your blogs on developing resilience. You could also consider sharing your experiences on TEDx Talks within your community and professional networks.

This chapter explored the different ways through which you can maintain your progress as you heal from trauma. Self-reflection, patience, and consistency are essential tools to help you manage setbacks and avoid relapsing. Your healing journey is continuous and may be filled with many mistakes you should be ready to learn from. Looking at your setbacks as opportunities that enhance growth will help you deal with them more resiliently. Also, remember to keep your mind focused on the future you desire while celebrating the successes you achieve along the way.

CONCLUSION

Certainly, trauma is not a one-size-fits-all kind of experience. The varying extent to which trauma affects people dramatically contributes to their different responses. Trauma can be classified into different types as follows:

- *Acute trauma* refers to cases where the trauma emanates from one stressful incident.
- *Chronic trauma*: In this case, the unpleasant, stressful, or scary event occurs repeatedly.
- *Complicated trauma*: This is a complex form where multiple stressful events repeat themselves.

Regardless of the type of trauma that you may be experiencing, the psychological and physical responses are similar. You may feel physical pain and headaches. Trauma may also trigger negative emotions such as fear, anxiety, regret, and blame. This may affect your self-esteem and general take on life, ultimately affecting your ability to complete tasks, communicate, collaborate with others, and form meaningful relationships, let alone sustain them. This partly explains why your healing journey should be focused on self-love, acceptance, and creating a safe environment.

Self-love describes the art of channeling some love, kindness, and compassion toward yourself. One of the most important things you should do as a self-love gesture is to speak positively about yourself, regardless of what you are going through. Accept what happened and make a solid choice to move on. You will also need a physical and social environment that is safe enough to encourage emotional healing.

While there is a lot that you can do to enhance your healing progress, you might need professional help, especially if you have been experiencing extreme effects of trauma for a long time. Therapists are professionally trained to help people going through different forms of trauma, including yours. They can offer customized assistance based on the factors that characterize your situation. Therapists can also suggest relevant methods for dealing with your trauma or refer you to doctors if needed.

The importance of resilience when dealing with trauma cannot be overstated. Resilience refers to the inner strength and ability to bounce back after adversity. Resilience helps you to see the traumatic situation as an opportunity for growth. Usually, resilience is the power behind PTG, as with well-known people like Oprah Winfrey, Walt Disney, and Michael Jordan. These people faced trauma and failures that could have taken them down for life, yet they returned even stronger. You also got this. Trust me!

Traumatic experiences can negatively affect relationships with others, even family members. This is more so if what you went through was perpetrated by people, as compared to events such as natural disasters. You may feel that your trust was betrayed, which is normal. However, shying away from all people could worsen your mental situation, making you vulnerable to more anxiety and depression. Remember, not everyone is against you. Identify people who can enhance positivity in your life and develop relationships with them.

Professional people like therapists could be an excellent way to start. You can also join support groups with people who have had similar experiences as yours. Also, make efforts to forgive the perpetrators while keeping yourself relatively safe. Embrace the company of others and remember that seeking help is a sign of strength, not weakness.

Self-care is an essential aspect of your healing process. It nourishes your physical, emotional, and psychological well-being, placing you in a better position to fight the negative effects of trauma. For example, regular exercise and eating healthy can reduce the production of stress hormones like cortisol. This improves your mood.

Please note that recovery from trauma is not a one-day event. It is a process that may take a lifetime, depending on the factors surrounding the trauma. You might have to deal with moments of relapse at some point. However, you should not hate yourself for that. Be kind to yourself and remember that your healing is a journey, not a single event.

Surround yourself with positivity by engaging with people who encourage you. Try to minimize the triggers whenever you can. For example, why not move away if a specific location is associated with the trauma? Sometimes, facing the triggers head-on could be the best option. Using the example we mentioned earlier, you could visit the place linked to the trauma more often. As time progresses, this will cultivate acceptance, the foundation for your healing.

As we conclude, you must keep the following main points at the tips of your fingers:

- Trauma affects each individual differently, and recovery is a personal journey.
- The healing process involves both physical and psychological strategies.

- Seeking professional help can be a critical step in the recovery process.
- Cultivating resilience and inner strength can significantly aid in overcoming trauma.
- Healthy relationships and self-care practices are vital components of trauma recovery.
- There's potential for personal growth even in the face of trauma.

The journey to recovering from trauma can be quite challenging, but this does not make it impossible. Access your reservoir of inner strength and start making the first step. Remember, "the journey of a thousand miles begins with one step." It's time to take the first step, whether acknowledging your trauma, seeking professional help, or implementing other strategies we discussed in this book. If you have already started your journey, please soldier on.

Take advantage of your story and turn it into PTG. You can still live a fulfilling life after all that you went through. I went through traumatic experiences, but I chose to make the best of it instead of letting them destroy me. Now, here I am, even better than before. If I could do this, so can you. Again, I emphasize that *you got this!*

Keeping the Healing Journey Alive

Now that you have gained valuable insights and tools to help you on your path to overcoming trauma, it's time to share your newfound knowledge and guide other readers to the same source of support.

By simply leaving your honest review of this book on Amazon, you will direct other individuals who are seeking healing and understanding towards the help they need. Your review can be a beacon of hope and guidance for someone else on their journey through trauma recovery.

Your contribution is invaluable. The journey of healing and understanding trauma is sustained and enriched when we share our experiences and insights. By leaving your review, you are playing a crucial role in this process, helping me to extend this support to others who are in need.

Thank you for your help in keeping this vital conversation about trauma and healing alive. You are making a real difference.

Click here to leave your review on Amazon

REFERENCES

Abdollahi, A., Alsaikhan, F., Nikolenko, D. A., Al-Gazally, M. E., Mahmudiono, T., Allen, K. A., & Abdullaev, B. (2022). Self-care behaviors mediate the relationship between resilience and quality of life in breast cancer patients. *BMC Psychiatry, 22*(1). https://doi.org/10.1186/s12888-022-04470-5

Ackerman, C. E. (2018, January 11). *7+ Trauma-focused cognitive behavioral therapy worksheets*. PositivePsychology.com. https://positivepsychology.com/trauma-focused-cognitive-behavioral-therapy/

AfterTrauma. (n.d.-a). *Shelly's story*. https://www.aftertrauma.org/survivors-stories/shellys-story

AfterTrauma. (n.d.-b). *Cristiana's story*. https://www.aftertrauma.org/survivors-stories/cristiana

Agnew, R. (2017). *General strain theory*. https://www.researchgate.net/publication/311251330_General_Strain_Theory

Ahmad, R. (2023, May 12). *Is the promotion of self-care and mindfulness on social media bettering our health?* LinkedIn. https://www.linkedin.com/pulse/promotion-self-care-mindfulness-social-media-bettering-rashid-ahmad

Al Jowf, G. I., Ahmed, Z. T., An, N., Reijnders, R. A., Ambrosino, E., Rutten, B. P. F., de Nijs, L., & Eijssen, L. M. T. (2022). A public health perspective of post-traumatic stress disorder. *International Journal of Environmental Research and Public Health, 19*(11), 6474. https://doi.org/10.3390/ijerph19116474

Alkan, M., & Meinck, S. (2016). The relationship between students' use of ICT for social communication and their computer and information literacy. *Large-Scale Assessments in Education, 4*(1). https://doi.org/10.1186/s40536-016-0029-z

American Psychological Association. (2017a). *Cognitive processing therapy (CPT)*. https://www.apa.org/ptsd-guideline/treatments/cognitive-processing-therapy

American Psychological Association. (2017b). *Eye movement desensitiza-*

tion and reprocessing (EMDR) therapy. https://www.apa.org/ptsd-guideline/treatments/eye-movement-reprocessing

American Psychological Association. (2017c). *Prolonged exposure (PE)*. https://www.apa.org/ptsd-guideline/treatments/prolonged-exposure

American Psychological Association. (2017d). *How do I find a good therapist?* https://www.apa.org/ptsd-guideline/patients-and-families/finding-good-therapist

American Psychological Association. (2017e, July 31). *Narrative exposure therapy (NET)*. https://www.apa.org/ptsd-guideline/treatments/narrative-exposure-therapy

American Psychological Association. (2020, February 1). *Building your resilience*. https://www.apa.org/topics/resilience/building-your-resilience

American Psychological Association. (2022, August). *Trauma*. https://www.apa.org/topics/trauma

Barclays Life Skills. (n.d.). *5 ways to find out what your strengths are*. https://barclayslifeskills.com/i-want-to-choose-my-next-step/school/5-ways-to-find-out-what-you-re-good-at/

Beidel, D. C., Frueh, B. C., Neer, S. M., & Lejuez, C. W. (2017). The efficacy of trauma management therapy: A controlled pilot investigation of a three-week intensive outpatient program for combat-related PTSD. *Journal of Anxiety Disorders, 50*, 23–32. https://doi.org/10.1016/j.janxdis.2017.05.001

Benjet, C., Bromet, E., Karam, E. G., Kessler, R. C., McLaughlin, K. A., Ruscio, A. M., Shahly, V., Stein, D. J., Petukhova, M., Hill, E., Alonso, J., Atwoli, L., Bunting, B., Bruffaerts, R., Caldas-de-Almeida, J. M., de Girolamo, G., Florescu, S., Gureje, O., Huang, Y., & Lepine, J. P. (2016). The epidemiology of traumatic event exposure worldwide: results from the World Mental Health Survey Consortium. *Psychological Medicine, 46*(02), 327–343. https://doi.org/10.1017/s0033291715001981

Calhoun, L. G., & Tedeschi, R. G. (2014). *Handbook of posttraumatic growth: Research and practice*. Routledge. https://books.google.co.za/books?hl=en&lr=&id=BHEABAAAQBAJ&oi=fnd&pg=PP1&dq=Calhoun+%26+Tedeschi

REFERENCES | 175

Campus Health. (2022, January 27). *Understanding mental health triggers.* https://campushealth.unc.edu/health-topic/understanding-mental-health-triggers/#:~:text=A%20trigger%20is%20a%20stimulus

Center for Health Care Strategies. (2018, November 8). *Medication trauma: What it is and how to help.* https://www.chcs.org/medication-trauma-what-it-is-and-how-to-help/

Center for Substance Abuse Treatment. (2014). *Trauma Awareness.* https://www.ncbi.nlm.nih.gov/books/NBK207203/

Cherry, K. (2017, December 31). *Know more. Live brighter.* Verywell Mind. https://www.verywellmind.com

Clear, J. (2013, July 19). *How to stop procrastinating by using the "Seinfeld strategy."* James Clear. https://jamesclear.com/stop-procrastinating-seinfeld-strategy

Collier, L. (2016, November). *Growth after trauma.* American Psychological Association. https://www.apa.org/monitor/2016/11/growth-trauma

D'Amore Mental Health. (2023, March 27). *Balancing self-care with life's obligations.* https://damorementalhealth.com/balancing-self-care-with-lifes-obligations/

Dr. Jamie Marich Home Page. (n.d.). Dr. Jamie Marich. https://www.drjamiemarich.com

Elam, T., & Taku, K. (2022). Differences between posttraumatic growth and resiliency: Their distinctive relationships with empathy and emotion recognition ability. *Frontiers in Psychology, 13.* https://doi.org/10.3389/fpsyg.2022.825161

Elias, R. (2023, January 17). *3 Things: Miracle on the Hudson.* Red Ventures. https://www.redventures.com/blog/3-things-miracle-on-the-hudson

Evidation. (n.d.). *Evidation | Real World Health Data.* https://evidation.com

Families for Depression Awareness. (2021, March 15). *12 Self-care tips for nurturing your body.* https://www.familyaware.org/12-self-care-tips-for-nurturing-your-body/

Fekete, E. M., & Deichert, N. T. (2022). A brief gratitude writing intervention decreased stress and negative affect during the COVID-19 pandemic. *Journal of Happiness Studies, 23*(6). https://doi.org/10.1007/s10902-022-00505-6

Fernández, A., & Green, M. (2019, October 3). *Tyler Perry opens up about healing from sexual abuse as a child: 'There Was a Lot of Anger.'* PEOPLE. https://people.com/movies/tyler-perry-on-healing-after-childhood-sexual-abuse/

FHE Health. (n.d.). *Statistics on mental trauma.* https://fherehab.com/trauma/statistics

Forbes Quotes. (n.d.). *Thoughts on the business of life.* https://www.forbes.com/quotes/11194/

Foy, C. (2020, June 25). *How a gratitude journal helped my trauma and PTSD.* FHE Health. https://fherehab.com/learning/gratitude-journaling-helps-trauma

GoodTherapy. (2019, May 15). *Self care in therapy.* https://www.goodtherapy.org/learn-about-therapy/issues/self-care

Great West Media. (2022, June 6). *The importance of balancing your life through self care.* MountainviewToday.ca. https://www.mountainviewtoday.ca/womens-wellness/the-importance-of-balancing-your-life-through-self-care-5448000

Greater Good in Education. (2019). *SEL for students: Self-awareness and self-management.* https://ggie.berkeley.edu/student-well-being/sel-for-students-self-awareness-and-self-management/

Gromer, S. (2022, December 13). *The vision board: A powerful tool and how it can help you achieve your goals.* Forbes. https://www.forbes.com/sites/forbescoachescouncil/2022/12/13/the-vision-board-a-powerful-tool-and-how-it-can-help-you-achieve-your-goals/

Hall, W. J., Chapman, M. V., Lee, K. M., Merino, Y. M., Thomas, T. W., Payne, B. K., Eng, E., Day, S. H., & Coyne-Beasley, T. (2015). Implicit racial/ethnic bias among health care professionals and its influence on health care outcomes: A systematic review. *American Journal of Public Health, 105*(12), 60–76. https://doi.org/10.2105/ajph.2015.302903

Harris, N. B. (2017, August 25). *Nadine Burke Harris: How does trauma affect a child's DNA?* NPR. https://www.npr.org/transcripts/545092982

Harvard Health Publishing. (2019). *Health information and medical information.* https://www.health.harvard.edu

Hetrick, S. E., Purcell, R., Garner, B., & Parslow, R. (2010). Combined pharmacotherapy and psychological therapies for post-traumatic stress disorder (PTSD). *Cochrane Database of Systematic Reviews, 7.* https://doi.org/10.1002/14651858.cd007316.pub2

Hood, J. (2018, December 20). *The importance of self-care after trauma.* Highland Springs. https://highlandspringsclinic.org/the-importance-of-self-care-after-trauma/

Huh, H. J., Kim, S.-Y., Yu, J. J., & Chae, J.-H. (2014). Childhood trauma and adult interpersonal relationship problems in patients with depression and anxiety disorders. *Annals of General Psychiatry, 13*(1). https://doi.org/10.1186/s12991-014-0026-y

Indeed. (2022, December 7). *How to identify your key strengths in the workplace.* https://www.indeed.com/career-advice/career-development/identifying-strengths

Inspire Malibu. (2021, January 21). *7 Famous people and celebrities with PTSD.* https://www.inspiremalibu.com/blog/dual-diagnosis/7-famous-people-and-celebrities-with-ptsd/

Jantz, Gregory. L. (2022, May 26). *6 Steps to rebuilding trust after betrayal.* Psychology Today. https://www.psychologytoday.com/intl/blog/hope-relationships/202205/6-steps-rebuilding-trust-after-betrayal

Jeffreys, M. (2022, October 6). *Clinician's guide to medications for PTSD.* U.S. Department of Veterans Affairs. https://www.ptsd.va.gov/professional/treat/txessentials/clinician_guide_meds.asp

Jin, Y., Bhattarai, M., Kuo, W., & Bratzke, L. C. (2022). Relationship between resilience and self-care in people with chronic conditions: A systematic review and meta-analysis. *Journal of Clinical Nursing.* https://doi.org/10.1111/jocn.16258

Joseph, S. (2009). Growth following adversity: Positive psychological perspectives on posttraumatic stress. *Psychological Topics, 18*(2), 335–344.

Kale, S. (2021, June 1). *"I know the power a young girl carries in her heart": The extraordinary life of Malala.* British Vogue. https://www.vogue.co.uk/news/article/malala-vogue-interview

Khiron Clinics. (2022, March 18). *The relationship between trauma and sleep.* https://khironclinics.com/blog/the-relationship-between-trauma-and-sleep/

KVC Health Systems. (2021, August 30). *Oprah Winfrey examines child-*

hood trauma and how to treat it. https://www.kvc.org/blog/oprah-winfrey-examines-childhood-trauma-and-how-to-treat-it/

Lanius, R. A., Terpou, B. A., & McKinnon, M. C. (2020). The sense of self in the aftermath of trauma: Lessons from the default mode network in posttraumatic stress disorder. *European Journal of Psychotraumatology, 11*(1), 1807703. https://doi.org/10.1080/20008198.2020.1807703

Lees, A. B. (2020, October 28). *7 Tools for managing traumatic stress.* National Alliance on Mental Illness. https://www.nami.org/Blogs/NAMI-Blog/October-2020/7-Tools-for-Managing-Traumatic-Stress

Let's Become Successful. (2021, April 29). *You Are More Than You Think | Les Brown | Motivational Speech* [Video]. YouTube. https://www.youtube.com/watch?v=pLNO_HoHWmw

Luckwaldt, J. H. (2022, February 2). *5 Famous people who were fired before becoming successful.* LiveAbout. https://www.liveabout.com/famous-people-who-were-fired-2060745

Luszczynska, A., Benight, C. C., & Cieslak, R. (2009). Self-efficacy and health-related outcomes of collective trauma. *European Psychologist, 14*(1), 51–62. https://doi.org/10.1027/1016-9040.14.1.51

Mayo Clinic. (2020, October 27). *Resilience: Build skills to endure hardship.* https://www.mayoclinic.org/tests-procedures/resilience-training/in-depth/resilience/art-20046311

Mikelson, B. (2018, April 13). *Book summary: The body keeps the score.* EMDR & Beyond. https://emdrandbeyond.com/blog/2018/4/13/trauma-book-club-summary-the-body-keeps-the-score

Mind. (2020, December). *What is dialectical behavioral therapy (DBT)?* https://www.mind.org.uk/information-support/drugs-and-treatments/talking-therapy-and-counselling/dialectical-behaviour-therapy-dbt/

Moore, C. (2019, June 19). *Resilience theory: What research articles in psychology teach us (+PDF).* PositivePsychology.com. https://positivepsychology.com/resilience-theory/

Moore, H. M., Eisenhauer, R. C., Killian, K. D., Proudfoot, N., Henriques, A. A., Congeni, J. A., & Reneker, J. C. (2016). The relationship between adherence behaviors and recovery time in adolescents after a sports-related concussion: An observational study. *International*

REFERENCES | 179

Journal of Sports Physical Therapy, 10(2), 225–233. https://www.ncbi.nlm.nih.gov/pmc/articles/PMC4387730/

My Mind Oasis. (2019, May 14). *What Is Self-care?* https://www.mymindoasis.com/blog/2019/5/14/what-is-self-care

National Center for PTSD. (2023, February 3). *How common is PTSD in adults?* https://www.ptsd.va.gov/understand/common/common_adults.asp

National Institute for Health and Care Excellence. (2018, December 5). *Recommendations | Post-traumatic stress disorder.* https://www.nice.org.uk/guidance/ng116/chapter/Recommendations#care-for-people-with-ptsd-and-complex-needs

National Institute of Mental Health. (2022, May). *Post-traumatic stress disorder.* https://www.nimh.nih.gov/health/topics/post-traumatic-stress-disorder-ptsd

Neff, K. (n.d.). *What is self-compassion?* Self-Compassion. https://selfcompassion.org/the-three-elements-of-self-compassion-2/

Nuffield Trust. (2023, April 27). *Adult substance misuse services.* https://www.nuffieldtrust.org.uk/resource/adult-substance-misuse-services-1?gclid

Nugent, N. R., Sumner, J. A., & Amstadter, A. B. (2014). Resilience after trauma: From surviving to thriving. *European Journal of Psychotraumatology, 5*(1), 25339. https://doi.org/10.3402/ejpt.v5.25339

Paulise, L. (2023, August 14). *The power of journaling and why it matters in your career.* Forbes. https://www.forbes.com/sites/lucianapaulise/2023/08/14/the-power-of-journaling-and-why-it-matters-in-your-career/?sh=5bf12d3a69aa

Payne, K. (2023, May 12). *How writing can help you heal and transform.* New Thinking. https://www.newthinking.com/health/how-writing-can-help-you-heal-and-transform

Perper, R. (2020, July 10). *How to be patient with yourself and others in a changing world.* Therapy Changes. https://therapychanges.com/blog/2020/07/how-to-be-patient-with-yourself-and-others-in-a-changing-world/

Perry, E. (2022, December 21). *Self-reflection: Learn how to better understand yourself.* BetterUp. https://www.betterup.com/blog/self-reflection

Porreca, T. (2021, June 4). *Celebrities who overcame drug addiction.* Resurgence Behavioral Health. https://resurgencebehavioralhealth.com/blog/6-celebrities-who-recovered-from-drug-addiction/

Proyer, R. T., Gander, F., Wellenzohn, S., & Ruch, W. (2015). Strengths-based positive psychology interventions: A randomized placebo-controlled online trial on long-term effects for signature strengths-vs. a lesser strengths intervention. *Frontiers in Psychology, 06.* https://doi.org/10.3389/fpsyg.2015.00456

Psychiatric Times. (2003, February 1). Combined therapy shows promise for PTSD. https://www.psychiatrictimes.com/view/combined-therapy-shows-promise-ptsd

Raypole, C. (2020, February 28). *Somatic experiencing: How it can help you.* Healthline. https://www.healthline.com/health/somatic-experiencing

Robinson, W. (2021, November 23). *15 Celebs who overcame traumatic childhoods.* Mom.com. https://mom.com/entertainment/celebrities-traumatic-childhoods/hilary-swank1

SAMHSA. (2022, September 27). *Trauma and violence.* https://www.samhsa.gov/trauma-violence

SAMHSA. (n.d.). *Trauma-informed care in behavioral health services.* https://store.samhsa.gov/sites/default/files/d7/priv/sma15-4420.pdf

Scribner, H. (2014, August 4). *9 Famous people who overcame childhood adversity.* Aberdeen News. https://www.aberdeennews.com/story/entertainment/2014/08/04/9-famous-people-who-overcame-childhood-adversity/44970799/

Sharma, P. (2023, August 5). *Embracing growth mindset: The key to thriving as entrepreneurs in the world.* LinkedIn. https://www.linkedin.com/pulse/embracing-growth-mindset-key-thriving-entrepreneurs-world-sharma

Sherin, J. E., & Nemeroff, C. B. (2011). Post-traumatic stress disorder: The neurobiological impact of psychological trauma. *Dialogues in Clinical Neuroscience, 13*(3), 263–278. https://www.ncbi.nlm.nih.gov/pmc/articles/PMC3182008/

Simons, J. (2022, July 20). *The story of Gabby Giffords' remarkable recovery.* Time. https://time.com/6198452/gabby-giffords-wont-back-down-tells-a-remarkable-story-of-recovery/

Solara Mental Health. (n.d.). *Water, depression, and anxiety.* https://solara mentalhealth.com/can-drinking-enough-water-help-my-depression-and-anxiety/

Southwick, S., Pietrzak, R., Tsai, J., Krystal, J., & Charney, D. (2011). *Resilience: An Update.* National Center for PTSD. https://www.ptsd.va.gov/publications/rq_docs/V25N4.pdf

Staglin, G. (2022, June 30). *Why global leaders must step up to address trauma now.* Forbes. https://www.forbes.com/sites/onemind/2022/06/30/why-global-leaders-must-step-up-to-address-trauma-now/?sh=62592f7130a1

Stanton, R. (2021, December 13). *7 Myths about trauma.* Counseling in Boston. https://counselinginboston.com/7-myths-about-trauma/

Stige, S. H., Binder, P.-E., & Veseth, M. (2017). The role of therapy in personal recovery – Trauma clients' use of resources to continue positive processes following group therapy. *Qualitative Social Work, 18*(1), 24–36. https://doi.org/10.1177/1473325017699264

Substance Abuse and Mental Health Services Administration. (2014). *Trauma-informed care in behavioral health services. Chapter 3: Understanding the impact of trauma.* https://www.ncbi.nlm.nih.gov/books/NBK207191/

Sudderth, C. (2023, May 26). *Trauma in online dating – A different perspective.* Brainz Magazine. https://www.brainzmagazine.com/post/trauma-in-online-dating-a-different-perspective

Tedeschi, R. G., & Calhoun, L. G. (1996). The posttraumatic growth inventory: Measuring the positive legacy of trauma. *Journal of Traumatic Stress, 9*(3), 455–472. https://doi.org/10.1002/jts.2490090305

The Bradley Center. (n.d.). *Bradley Center success stories.* https://thebradleycenter.org/success-stories/

The Burke Foundation. (2019, April 25). *Adverse childhood experiences (ACEs).* https://burkefoundation.org/what-drives-us/adverse-childhood-experiences-aces/

The Human Condition. (2022, January 15). *Emotional self-care: Importance, benefits, practices.* https://thehumancondition.com/emotional-self-care-importance-benefits-practices/

The National Council for Behavioral Health. (n.d.). *How to manage trauma*. https://www.thenationalcouncil.org/wp-content/uploads/ 2022/08/Trauma-infographic.pdf

The Wellness Society. (n.d.). *76 Healing trauma quotes and affirmations + free printable affirmation cards.* https://thewellnesssociety.org/76-healing-cptsd-quotes-and-affirmations/

Theisen, A. (2021, December 8). *Is a sense of belonging important?* Mayo Clinic Health System. https://www.mayoclinichealthsystem.org/hometown-health/speaking-of-health/is-having-a-sense-of-belonging-important

Trauma Survivors Network. (2023). *Survivor stories.* https://www.traumasurvivorsnetwork.org/pages/survivor-stories

Trauma Survivors Network. (n.d.). *Lisa's story.* https://www.traumasurvivorsnetwork.org/pages/1194

U.S. Department of Veterans Affairs. (2022, November 8). *Relationships.* https://www.ptsd.va.gov/family/effect_relationships.asp

University of Pacific. (2022, May 12). *"Your attitude, not your aptitude, will determine your altitude."* – Zig Ziglar. https://pacific.edu.ni/your-attitude-not-your-aptitude-will-determine-your-altitude-zig-ziglar/

Utah State University. (2023). *Effective Communication Skills: "I" Messages and Beyond.* https://extension.usu.edu/relationships/research/effective-communication-skills-i-message-and-beyond

Watkins, B. (2019, March 13). *Thomas Edison's theorem for success.* Medium. https://medium.com/cry-mag/thomas-edisons-theorem-for-success-b96591bf7dd1

Werner, K. H., Jazaieri, H., Goldin, P. R., Ziv, M., Heimberg, R. G., & Gross, J. J. (2012). Self-compassion and social anxiety disorder. *Anxiety, Stress & Coping, 25*(5), 543–558. https://doi.org/10.1080/10615806.2011.608842

White, W. A. (2023, August 15). *Enjoy the journey by celebrating the small victories.* Forbes. https://www.forbes.com/sites/forbesbusinesscouncil/2023/08/15/enjoy-the-journey-by-celebrating-the-small-victories/?sh=6485c6c45bcf

Williams, R. (2021, September 6). *Positive life lessons from 8 celebrities.* Lifeism. https://lifeism.co/positive-life-lessons-from-8-celebrities

Williams, Z. (2021, September 20). *Trauma, trust, and triumph: Psychiatrist Bessel van der Kolk on how to recover from our deepest pain.* The

Guardian. https://www.theguardian.com/society/2021/sep/20/trauma-trust-and-triumph-psychiatrist-bessel-van-der-kolk-on-how-to-recover-from-our-deepest-pain

Yao, Z.-F., & Hsieh, S. (2019). Neurocognitive mechanism of human resilience: A conceptual framework and empirical review. *International Journal of Environmental Research and Public Health, 16*(24), 5123. https://doi.org/10.3390/ijerph16245123

YourDOST. (n.d.). *10 Incredibly famous people who found success after getting fired.* https://yourdost.com/blog/2017/06/celebrities-who-were-fired-before-becoming-succesful.html?q=/blog/2017/06/celebrities-who-were-fired-before-becoming-succesful.html&

Printed in Great Britain
by Amazon